Making Headway
Upper-Intermediate

Phrasal Verbs and Idioms

Graham Workman

Oxford University Press

Oxford University Press
Great Clarendon Street, Oxford OX2 6DP

Oxford New York
Auckland Bangkok Buenos Aires Cape Town
Chennai Dar es Salaam Delhi Hong Kong
Istanbul Karachi Kolkata Kuala Lumpur
Madrid Melbourne Mexico City Mumbai
Nairobi São Paulo Shanghai Singapore
Taipei Tokyo Toronto

with an associated company in Berlin

OXFORD and OXFORD ENGLISH are trade marks of
Oxford University Press

ISBN 0 19 435509 8

© Oxford University Press 1993

First published 1993
Sixth impression 2002

No unauthorized photocopying

Typeset by Wyvern Typesetting Limited,
Bristol

Printed in Hong Kong

Acknowledgements

Illustrations by
Kevin Baverstock
Caroline Church
David Murray
Nigel Paige
Bill Piggins

Location photography by
Rob Judges

The publishers would like to thank the
following for their permission to
reproduce
photographs:

Barnaby's Picture Library
Channel 4 News
Format Partners Photo Library
Impact Photos Ltd
Network Photographers
The Telegraph Colour Library Ltd

Contents

Foreword

Students of English realize very early on in their learning career that prepositions present a problem. They collocate with nouns, adjectives, past participles, and verbs, without rules or logic. Students simply have to learn that *interested* is followed by *in*, and *good* is followed by *at*, and *go home* has no preposition. Multi-word verbs, or phrasal verbs as they are often referred to, present a very special problem. English can make verb and particle (preposition or adverb) combinations easily and freely. The word *particle* has been used throughout this book, in order to avoid having to make the adverb/preposition distinction (to most students, the word after the verb in a multi-word verb is always a preposition). Multi-word verbs exist throughout the language. They express everyday actions such as *Turn on the light*; they can also have a variety of meanings such as *Things worked out well, We worked out the problem, She worked out in the gym, I've never been able to work him out*, and *The final price works out at £10*.

Given the complexity of the area, the surprise is that learners are very keen to master it. They seem to sense that multi-word verbs are a vital component of English, and spoken English in particular. There is also the feeling that an understanding of common idioms will increase their comprehension, though most students instinctively avoid trying to produce them. The best time to address these areas is at upper-intermediate and advanced levels, when students already have a certain grammatical and lexical foundation.

This book goes a long way to helping students to unravel the complexity of multi-word verbs, preposition and adverb collocations, and idiomatic expressions. Students will find staged guidance in understanding the systems, and are given a variety of exercise practice in recognition and production. *Phrasal Verbs and Idioms* will find its place in self-access centres, for learners to study on their own; and teachers will welcome the texts, listenings, explanations, and exercises, which have clear aims and are highly accessible for thorough classroom exploitation.

John and Liz Soars
Series editors

Introduction

Who this book is for

This book is for students who are studying *Headway Upper-Intermediate* or any other coursebook at a similar level. It can also be used by students who are preparing for Cambridge FCE examinations.

How the book is organized

The materials in each unit are organized around themes such as work, health, holidays, accommodation, family relationships, etc. The units are relatively free-standing and can therefore be used to supplement existing coursebooks. The book is also designed to provide students with an idea of how multi-word verbs work, so there is some advantage in working through the units systematically. Some of the later units recycle multi-word verbs used in earlier units.

The book contains over 200 multi-word verbs. They have been selected according to the theme of each unit, as well as level of difficulty and usefulness. Four main types of multi-word verb are introduced, and various types of practice exercises are provided for consolidation work.

How to use the book

To the teacher

1   Use the Introductory unit before any other units in the book. This should take about 45–60 minutes of classroom time. All the remaining units contain enough material for approximately 60–90 minutes of teaching.

2   The units follow a reasonably consistent pattern:

The **Preparation** section is designed as a *brief* lead in to the theme of the unit, not lasting more than five minutes.
The **Presentation** is usually a listening or reading text, followed by an exercise in which multi-word verbs are matched with their definitions.
The **Drills** provide controlled oral practice of the new multi-word verbs, but they can also be used as prompts for later revision work, or written controlled practice.
The **Practice** section gives students the opportunity to use the multi-word verbs to talk about their own experiences and ideas. There are also practice exercises for prepositions and idiomatic expressions.
How multi-word verbs work deals with the systems of multi-word verbs and the meaning of some particles.

5

What's the answer? is designed to check that students have understood the important differences between a few multi-word verbs. It can be used as a game or revision activity.

The **Jokes** provide some light relief. They are related to the theme of the unit and illustrate some humorous uses of multi-word verbs.

The **Writing** section provides further written consolidation of the language covered in the unit.

3   It is important that students are given some activities for revising the multi-word verbs they learn in the book. One simple revision activity is to put students into pairs and tell student A to read the definitions of some the multi-word verbs while student B says what the multi-word verb is. Alternatively, some multi-word verbs can be put into a *'Find someone who'* activity as a warmer for the start of a lesson (e.g. 'Find someone who sets off for school very early in the morning'). Students can be asked to act out some of the dialogues on the tape, and their spoken or written errors with multi-word verbs can be used in a *Grammar Auction* game.

To the student working independently

1   Read and listen to the presentation reading and listening texts, using the cassette and the tapescripts. Then do the exercises which follow.

2   Test yourself by listening and responding to the drills on the cassette. Alternatively, use the tapescript of the drills – you can cover up the answer and see if you produce the right response.

3   Work through the written exercises in the book and check your answers in the Answer key.

4   Find a friend to practise the spoken exercises with, or write out what you would say.

5   Do the free writing activities and then find someone who can correct them.

Introductory unit

Multi-word verbs are verbs that combine with one or two particles (a preposition and/or an adverb).

I'm **looking for** my keys. Have you seen them?
(verb + preposition)

Look out! There's a car coming!
(verb + adverb)

A snob is someone who **looks down on** people of a lower social class.
(verb + adverb + preposition)

If the addition of the particle(s) changes the meaning of the verb, it is usually called a *phrasal verb* because it has the meaning of a phrase. However, there are so many different types of phrasal verbs that it is easier to call all combinations of verb + particle(s) *multi-word verbs*.

Literal meaning
Look at the following example, where the verb and particle keep their separate literal meaning.

He **looked up** and saw a plane.

Here the meaning of the verb and the particle have not changed.

He **looked up** = He looked + up (in the direction of the sky).

Non-literal meaning
Sometimes the addition of the particle(s) creates a multi-word verb that has a different meaning.

He **looked up** all the new words in the dictionary.

In this sentence, *look up* = to find information in a reference book.

1 The first three example sentences on this page all have multi-word verbs with non-literal meanings. Look at them and decide what they mean.

to look for someone/something = _____
to look out = _____
to look down on someone = _____

2 Look at the verbs below. Write L next to them if they have a literal meaning and N if they have a non-literal meaning. If the meaning is non-literal, say what it is. For example:

☐L He **held up** the World Cup and everybody cheered.
☐N Armed robbers **held up** the bank and escaped with £50,000.
(to hold up = to rob a place or person, usually with a gun)

a. ☐ He *ran out of* the building to escape the fire.
b. ☐ We've *run out of* coffee. Would you like tea instead?
c. ☐ He *looked through* the window to see if she was at home.
d. ☐ She *put* her bag *on* the desk and opened it.
e. ☐ The police are *looking into* the cause of the accident.
f. ☐ The car *went over* the cliff and crashed into the sea.
g. ☐ Can you *look through* my homework to see if it's correct?
h. ☐ He *put* the radio *on* so he could listen to the news.
i. ☐ She *looked into* the room but couldn't see him.
j. ☐ Can you *go over* your explanation once more, please?

Semi-literal meaning
The meaning of some multi-word verbs is completely different from the separate literal meanings of the verb and particle.

*I want to **give up** smoking.* = I want to stop smoking.

However, some multi-word verbs have a semi-literal meaning: the basic meaning of the verb remains the same, but the particle adds its own particular meaning.

*We decided to **drive on**.* = We decided to continue driving.

In this example, the particle *on* gives the idea of *continuing with something*

The meaning of particles

Some particles can have a general meaning when combined with a certain group of verbs. For example, the particle *round* can be used to give the meaning of *visiting someone informally*.

*You can **call round** any time. We'll always be pleased to see you.*
*Would you like to **come round** on Saturday? We'll be in all day.*
*Let's **ask** Ann and Mark **round** for a meal next week.*
*I'll **drop round** and see him on my way home from work.*
*She isn't here at the moment. She's **gone round** to see the woman next door.*

3 What is the general meaning of the particle *over* in all the examples below?

*The wind was so strong it **blew over** the garden wall.*
*As he entered the room he **tripped over** and fell onto the floor.*
*The car **knocked over** a man on a bicycle.*

*She placed her bicycle carefully against the wall but it **fell over**.*
*Our cat was **run over** by a lorry last week.*
*The little girl **pushed** him **over** and he fell onto some glass.*

The frequency and style of multi-word verbs

I can't put up with this noise any longer.

(informal spoken English)

Multi-word verbs are frequently used in everyday spoken English and they usually have an informal style. Quite often there is no single word which has exactly the same meaning as the multi-word verb, but for some of them there is a Latin-based verb which has an equivalent meaning. However, these Latin-based verbs tend to be used in more formal contexts.

> This letter is to inform you that we are not prepared to tolerate any further disturbance from your cassette player and will take appropriate legal action if it continues.

(formal written English)

When a more formal style is required, as in an official report or announcement, non-literal multi-word verbs are usually replaced with more formal words and expressions. However, sometimes there is little difference in the degree of formality between multi-word verbs and their equivalents.

*I've **picked up** a cold. = I've **caught** a cold.*

Multiple meanings

The same multi-word verb can have several different meanings:

1 I finally *worked out* the answer to the problem.
2 I am fit and strong because I *work out* in the gymnasium for an hour every day.
3 I *worked out* how much it would cost me to travel across Europe by train.
4 He's a very strange person. I can't *work* him *out*.

4 Match the different meanings of *work out* in the sentences above with the definitions below.

a. to do physical exercises
b. to understand someone
c. to calculate something
d. to find a solution to something

Word order

Each multi-word verb has its own rule for word order. Multi-word verbs which have more than one meaning can have several word order rules. Some descriptions of these rules are too complex to be useful, but there are four basic types which cover most multi-word verbs.

9

The four basic types

Type 1 multi-word verbs

Some multi-word verbs are intransitive (i.e. they don't take an object). We can use these multi-word verbs in a sentence on their own or continue the sentence in any way we like in order to add further information:

*John **called round**.*
*John **called round** last night.*
*John **called round** to see you.*
*John **called round** because he wanted to borrow some sugar.*

It is impossible to separate the verb and the particle.

Not ~~John called last night round~~.
Not ~~John called to see you round~~.

> Type 1 multi-word verbs: intransitive + inseparable

Type 1 multi-word verbs are written in a dictionary with nothing after them (i.e. without *someone* or *something*) to show they are intransitive and inseparable: *to call round*.

Type 2 multi-word verbs

Type 2 multi-word verbs are transitive (i.e. they take a direct object) and separable (i.e. it is possible to separate the verb and the particle). For example, these two sentences have the same meaning:

*He **looked up** the word in the dictionary.*
*He **looked** the word **up** in the dictionary.*

If an object pronoun is used (*me/you/him/her/it/us/them*), the particle must always come after the object pronoun:

*He **looked** it **up**.   Not ~~He looked up it~~.*

In other words, you have to separate the verb and the particle when you use an object pronoun.

> Type 2 multi-word verbs: transitive + separable

look up	the word	
look	the word	up
	it	

Type 2 multi-word verbs are written with *someone* and/or *something* between the verb and the particle to show they can be separated: *to look something up*.

5 Write your own example sentences with the following Type 2 multi-word verbs.

> to work something out   to switch something off
> to turn something on   to run someone over
> to ask someone round   to fill something in

Use both noun objects and pronoun objects to show that the particle can be separated from the verb.

*I **worked out** the meaning of the word from context. I **worked** it **out**.*

Type 3 multi-word verbs

Type 3 multi-word verbs are transitive and it is impossible to separate the verb and the particle by the noun object or the pronoun object:

*I'm **looking for** my keys.   Not ~~I'm looking my keys for~~.*
I'm **looking for** them.   Not ~~I'm looking them for~~.

> Type 3 multi-word verbs: transitive + inseparable

look for | my keys
         | them

Type 3 multi-word verbs are written with *someone* and/or *something* after the particle to show that they are transitive and inseparable: *to look for someone/something*.

6 Look at the following sentences and decide if the multi-word verbs are Type 1, Type 2, or Type 3.

a. I haven't got time to read your report now, so I'll look through it later.
b. The children woke up several times in the night.
c. I don't like getting up very early in the morning.
d. It's very dark in here. Can you put the light on, please?
e. I work out in a gymnasium because it helps to reduce stress.
f. She went over it several times but I still didn't understand.
g. The wind was so strong it almost blew me over.
h. I think the committee should look into it.
i. I'm afraid I've broken the vase. I knocked it over while I was polishing the table.
j. On Saturday we'll drop round to see if you need anything.

Type 4 multi-word verbs

Type 4 multi-word verbs are always transitive and have two particles which are inseparable.

*He looks **down on** other people.*   Not ~~He looks down other people on~~.
                                         Not ~~He looks other people down on~~.
*He **looks down on** them.*   Not ~~He looks down them on~~.
                                         Not ~~He looks them down on~~.

> Type 4 multi-word verbs: transitive + two inseparable particles

---

Type 4 multi-word verbs are written with *someone* and/or *something* after the two particles: *to look down on someone.*

Someone *and/or* *something*

Some multi-word verbs can be used to talk about people (*someone*) and things (*something*) without any difference in meaning. In a dictionary these verbs have *someone/something* after them. However, some multi-word verbs change their meaning depending on whether they are talking about people or things. For example, *to get on with someone* and *to get on with something* are not the same:

*Do you **get on with** your neighbours?* = Do you have a good relationship with your neighbours?

*How are you **getting on with** your studies?* = What progress are you making with your studies?

More than one type

A few multi-word verbs can behave like Type 1 *and* Type 4:

How do you get on with your boss?	(Type 4)
We get on very well.	(Type 1)
How are you getting on with your studies?	(Type 4)
I'm getting on very well at the moment.	(Type 1)

A few others can behave like Type 1 *and* Type 3:

He tripped over and hurt his knee.	(Type 1)
He tripped over the carpet.	(Type 3)

7   Put the following multi-word verbs under the headings below.

to get on (with something)   to put up with someone/something
to hold something up   to get on (with someone)
to run out (of something)   to push someone/something over
to fall over (something)   to come round

Type 1   **Type 2**   **Type 3**   **Type 4**

1 Getting down to work

Preparation

Work in pairs. Do you have any of the following study problems? If you do, discuss them with your partner.

In class	Outside class
☐ It's difficult to concentrate.	☐ You have nowhere quiet to study.
☐ You can't follow the lesson.	☐ You lack self-discipline.
☐ You don't like the subject.	☐ It's difficult to begin studying.
☐ Other students are much better than you.	☐ You don't have enough time.
☐ Other problems (What?)	☐ Other problems (What?)

Presentation

George had problems with studying, so he wrote to a magazine problem page for advice. Find out what his study problems are and tell your partner about four of them.

Dear Marjorie

I'm having problems with my studies at school. I find it difficult to get down to work in the evenings and I can't concentrate on anything at the moment. I spend most of my time listening to records or watching TV instead of doing my homework. The other students in my class are much better than I am and I have difficulty in keeping up with them. I sometimes have problems with following the lessons as well. I can't always take down the important things my teacher says because I write so slowly. She has told me that I'm falling behind with my studies. I'm not good at writing essays and I usually hand in my homework late because I put off doing it until the last minute. So I often have to invent silly excuses to explain why I haven't done the work.

I'm sure I'm not going to get through my final exams in June. I scraped through the mock exams last February with 54% – all the other students passed with flying colours. I'm now so far behind that I don't know how I'm going to catch up with them. My teacher spent some time going through my homework with me but she found so many mistakes that I felt even more depressed. What do you suggest I do?

Yours desperately

George.

Work with your partner. Underline the multi-word verbs in the letter and try to work out what they mean.

Checking understanding

1 Match the multi-word verbs in A with the definitions in B.

A	B
1 to get down to doing something	a. to be behind with something, not at the level expected
2 to keep up with someone/something	b. to start work on something
3 to take something down	c. to postpone, to decide to do something at a later date
4 to fall behind (with something)	d. to pass an exam or test
5 to hand something in	e. to check that something is correct, to examine something
6 to put something off	f. to reach the same standard or position as someone else
7 to get through (something)	g. to give something to someone in a position of authority
8 to scrape through (something)	h. to remain at the same standard or position as someone else
9 to catch up (with someone/something)	i. to record in writing what someone is saying
10 to go through something	j. to pass an exam but with a very low grade

2 Look at the pictures. How are the horses doing? Complete the sentences below, using multi-word verbs.

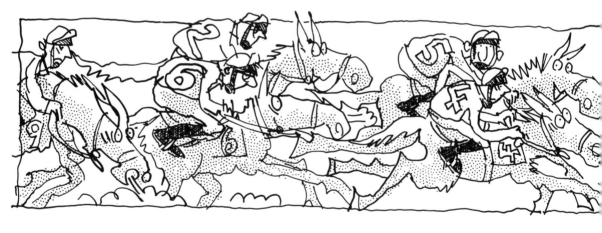

1 Number 9 is _____ .

2 Number 6 is _____ number 2.

3 Number 5 is _____ number 4.

Drills

T.1

Listen to the sentences on the tape. Replace the verbs in each sentence with a multi-word verb from this unit, and repeat the sentence. After a pause you will hear the correct multi-word verb. After another pause you will hear the whole sentence.

Practice

1   Ask your partner the questions below. Try to use the multi-word verbs from this unit in your questions and answers.

A *How are you **getting on with** your studies?*
B *At the moment I'm **falling behind** a little, so I'll have to work harder to **catch up with** the rest of the class.*

a. How are you getting on with your studies?
b. What things do you write down in lessons?
c. Do you always do your homework immediately?
d. How do you check there are no mistakes in your work before you give it to your teacher?
e. How do you think you will do in your future exams?

2   Fill in the gaps below.

| to have difficulty _____ (do*ing*) something |
| to have problems _____ (do*ing*) something |
| to concentrate _____ (do*ing*) something |

| to be good/quite good |
| not good/bad   _____   (do*ing*) something |
| awful/hopeless |

3   Use the phrases in the boxes above to write some sentences about yourself. Then discuss them with your partner. Find out how many things you have in common.

A *I'm good at using computers and learning languages. What are you good at?*
B *I'm quite good at using computers, but I have problems with learning languages. I have difficulty in remembering the grammar rules!*

Idiomatic expressions

4   What does *The other students passed with flying colours* mean?
How would you say the same thing in your own language?

5 Work with your partner. Look at the expressions in *italics* and work out what they mean. Do you have similar expressions in your own language?

The written exam was difficult, but the oral exam was *a piece of cake.*
It will be easier if we work on this exercise together. *Two heads are better than one.*
Her teacher told her that if she wanted to catch up with the rest of the class and pass her exams, she would have to *burn the midnight oil* for several weeks.
I passed the exam *by the skin of my teeth.* The pass mark was 50% and I got 51%.
When I went to school the teachers used to make us *learn* poems *by heart.*
On one occasion I *learnt* a whole speech *parrot fashion* – I didn't understand a word of it.

6 Now discuss the following questions:

– What exams have you passed by the skin of your teeth or with flying colours?
– How useful is it to learn things parrot fashion?
– What things did you learn by heart at school? Can you still remember them?
– What are the arguments for and against learning things by heart?
– What do you think is a good way to learn multi-word verbs and idiomatic expressions?

How multi-word verbs work
The particle *through* can be used with some verbs to give the idea of *reading something* (sometimes quickly) in order to find information.

go through something	read through something	look through something

The particle *through* can also be used with some verbs to give the idea of *completing something,* such as an exam or test.

scrape through something   get through something
sail through something (to succeed in something without any difficulty)

Through can also be used to describe completing a process of thought.

think something through (to consider something in detail in order to understand it completely and then make a decision or take action)

The particle *down* can be used with some verbs to give the idea of *recording something in writing.*

write something down/put something down (to write or type words or numbers)	copy something down (to write down something that is spoken or displayed)
get something down (to manage to write down what someone is saying, usually with difficulty)	note something down (to make short notes about something so they can be referred to later)

7 Write the correct idiomatic expression under each of the pictures.

a. It's very easy!

b. Let's do this together!

c. Exams soon!

d. Fantastic!

8 Complete the sentences below with suitable multi-word verbs. Sometimes more than one answer is possible.

ADVICE ON DOING EXAMS

Many people don't _____ their exams or only manage to _____ them with a very low grade because they make two simple mistakes: they often choose the wrong questions to answer and they don't plan their essays in sufficient detail. So here is some advice.

1 When you get your exam paper, _____ all the questions before you choose which ones you want to answer.

2 When you have done this, _____ on a spare piece of paper any relevant ideas that come to mind.

3 Next, _____ what you want to say in your essay before you begin writing.

4 Make a plan and then start your essay.

This advice does not guarantee you will _____ all your exams without any difficulties at all, but it will help you to avoid making major mistakes.

What's the answer?

What is the difference between *to keep up with* and *to catch up with?*

Jokes

Teacher *Smith, you should have been here at nine o'clock!*
Smith *Why, what happened?*

Mother *How are you getting on with your exams?*
Son *Not bad. The questions are easy. It's the answers I have problems with!*

Speaking

Work with your partner. Take turns to use rolecards A and B. Give yourself time to prepare your role and think about the multi-word verbs and expressions you might use.

Rolecard A

You have the following problems with your studies:
– difficulty in starting to study
– problems with doing homework
– the level of the other students in your class
– lack of progress
– worries about the exams in June
– any other problems

Talk to your partner and ask for advice.
You can decide to accept the advice that he or she gives:
Yes, that's a good idea.
Or you can reject it: *That's easier said than done.*

Rolecard B

Your partner is going to tell you about his or her problems with studying.
Give as much helpful advice as you can
When giving advice, you can say:
*Have you tried . . . + **ing**?*
*Why don't you try . . . + **ing**?*

Writing

Write a letter replying to the one on page 13. Give George advice about his study problems. Remember to sound encouraging!

2 Looking round a flat

Preparation

Work in pairs. Discuss the following questions.

– How would you improve the decoration of your classroom?
– Look at the picture of the flat below. What changes would you make to improve it?

FLAT
FOR SALE
One-bedroom
flat, needs
some attention,
lots of potential,
convenient
location, vacant
possession.
Available now.

Presentation

Ann saw the advertisement for the flat above. She contacted the estate agent and asked to look round it. He showed her round it the following day.

– What do you think Ann will say when she looks round the flat?
– What do you think the estate agent will say?

T.2a

Now listen to their conversation and answer the following questions.

1 What needs doing to the flat?
2 Does she decide to buy it?

Checking understanding

put something in	put something up	see to something
talk something over	throw something out	do something up
take something out	come off	think something over
move in		

1 Replace the words in *italics* in the sentences below with the multi-word verbs in the box. The first one has been done for you.

   a. Nothing has been done to this flat for a long time. It needs new curtains and a new carpet. The doors and walls also need painting. It needs <u>doing up</u> (*decorating/renovating*).
   b. The wallpaper was very old and _____ (*wasn't sticking to/attached to*) the walls.
   c. The fireplace was old and ugly, so they _____ (*removed it*).
   d. The house was cold and damp, so they had central heating _____ (*installed*).
   e. There was nowhere to put any books, so they decided to _____ (*fix in place*) some shelves.
   f. The carpets were old and full of holes, so he _____ (*disposed of them by putting them in the dustbin*).
   g. There was a serious problem with the roof. The rain was coming in and making everything wet. It needed _____ (*repairing/dealing with*) immediately.
   h. Before I make a decision I need to talk to my husband about it and see what he thinks. I must _____ (*discuss it*) with him.
   i. We would like to _____ (*start living there*) as soon as possible.
   j. It's a good idea, but I need time to _____ (*consider it carefully*) before I make a decision.

◀ T.2a

2 Now listen to the tape again and check your answers.

Drills

T.2b

You are looking round the flat with Ann. Agree with everything she says, using the multi-word verbs in the prompts.

Practice

T.2c

1 The picture opposite shows a house in good condition. Listen to a description of how the house used to look before it was done up. Make notes and then report back on the changes that have been made.

Example
The roof has been seen to.

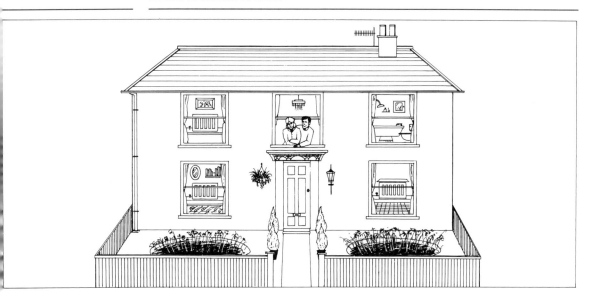

need + gerund

This construction is passive in meaning.

*The roof needs **seeing to**. = The roof needs **to be seen to**.*

2   Complete the sentences below. The first one has been done for you.

a. That ugly fireplace needs   *taking out.*
                                 _____
                                 to be taken out.

b. The house   _____
                     _____

c. Those shelves   _____
                         _____

d. That old table   _____
                          _____

e. The flat   _____
                    _____

f. The central heating   _____
                               _____

Idiomatic expressions

3 What do the following expressions mean? When would you use them?

1 Home, sweet home.
2 An Englishman's home is his castle.
3 Make yourself at home.
4 It's home from home.

How would you express the same ideas in your own language?

4 Complete the following sentences with a suitable idiomatic expression.

a. Come in and have a seat. I want you to feel you can behave as if you were in your house. So _____ while I make a cup of tea.
b. They made me feel very welcome. It was like being in my own house. It was _____.
c. He had enjoyed travelling round the world and seeing different places, but at last he had returned. He walked towards his house and thought '_____'.
d. I can do what I want in my own house. You know what they say, _____.

How multi-word verbs work

5 Replace the noun objects with pronoun objects (*it/them*) in the following sentences.

Shall I fill in this form? → *Shall I **fill** it **in**?*

a. I'd like to talk over my financial position.
b. Did you throw out those old newspapers?
c. They've decided to put off the wedding.
d. We're going to do up the kitchen.
e. I'd like more time to think over your offer.
f. I didn't take down his telephone number.
g. Did you hand in your homework?
h. Can you help me put up these pictures?

6 Now decide which words are stressed in the sentences with pronoun objects. Practise saying them. What is the stress rule in these examples?

T.2d

7 Now listen and check your answers.

What's the answer?

What's the difference between *to take something out* and *to throw something out*?

Jokes

> *This is a quiet, happy neighbourhood with dogs and children riding bicycles.*

DOG NEEDS HOME. EATS ANYTHING, LOVES CHILDREN.

Speaking

1 The estate agent is showing another client round the flat. Practise the dialogue with your partner, using the prompts below.

Estate agent	Client
① *Describe the flat – it's not in perfect condition!*	*Comment on the wallpaper and the old carpet.* ②
③ *Agree the flat needs decorating. Say it would look nice with new shelves, curtains, etc.*	*Say the flat is cold and damp, and the fireplace is ugly.* ④
⑤ *Say central heating could be installed.*	*Comment on the hole in the ceiling and the broken window.* ⑥
⑦ *Say that repairs will be done.*	*Say you are interested in the flat but need to discuss it with someone.* ⑧
⑨ *Say he or she can occupy the flat immediately.*	*Say you need time to consider it.* ⑩
⑪ *Say other people are interested in it.*	*Say you will get back to him, and thank him for his help. Say goodbye.* ⑫

2 *There's no place like home.* Do you agree? Why? Discuss with your partner.

Writing

Ann talked to her husband Tony about the flat and they discussed whether or not they should buy it. Write the dialogue, using language from this unit.

3 Healthy body, healthy mind

Preparation

Work in pairs. Discuss the following questions.
- What do you understand by the expression 'Healthy body, healthy mind'?
- Look at the picture. Why do you think these patients want to see the doctor?

Presentation

T.3a

Listen to the four patients talking to the doctor. Make notes about each of them under the headings below.

Patient	Symptoms	Diagnosis	Treatment
1 Mr Rich Brown			
2 Ms Teresa Green			
3 Mrs Lily White			
4 Mr Ivor Rose			

Checking understanding

T.3b

Listen to the sentences with the multi-word verbs in A. Match the verbs in A with the definitions in B.

A	B
1 to get over something	a. to increase in weight or size
2 to come/go down with something	b. to recover from an illness, shock, or surprise
3 to get through an amount of something	c. to develop the symptoms of an illness or disease
4 to pick something up	d. to use a quantity of something such as food or money
5 to cut something out	e. to reduce something, to consume less of something
6 to put on an amount of something	f. to develop an interest in something as a hobby or profession
7 to take something up	g. to recover consciousness
8 to cut down (on) (something)	h. to stop doing/using something
9 to pass out	i. to catch an illness
10 to come round	j. to faint, to lose consciousness for a short time because of lack of food or air, or because of shock

Drills

T.3c

Listen and respond to the prompts.

Practice

Idiomatic expressions

1 The following expressions were used in the conversations with the doctor. What do you think they mean?

1 That's easier said than done.
2 to feel off colour
3 to burn the candle at both ends
4 to take it easy
5 to be/feel worn out
6 to be/feel run down
7 to feel under the weather
8 to feel as right as rain

2   Which of the expressions in **1** could you use in the following situations?

a. Your friend has been working very hard and you think she needs a rest.
b. You're at work but you don't feel very well and you want to go home.
c. Someone gives you advice which is very difficult to follow.
d. You want to tell your friend she'll soon recover from her illness.
e. Your friend is looking tired. He works during the day and stays up late at night.

3   Work in pairs. Take turns to ask and answer the questions below. Try to use the multi-word verbs and expressions from this unit.

a. Do you smoke? If yes, how many cigarettes do you smoke a day?
b. Have you ever tried stopping or reducing the amount you smoke?
c. Have you changed your eating habits recently (for example, reduced the amount of fatty food you eat, or gone on a diet)?
d. Would you consider doing any of the following activities to keep fit?
   ☐ jogging   ☐ aerobics   ☐ cycling   ☐ golf   ☐ other
e. Are you ever out of breath? If yes, when?
f. Do you ever feel worn out or run down? If yes, when?
g. Have you ever fainted? If yes, explain what happened.
h. When was the last time you did not feel well? What was wrong with you?
i. When did you last have a cold? How long did it take you to recover from it?
j. How healthy do you think you are?

out of
*I'm always **out of** breath.*
*My husband is **out of** work.*

Work with your partner. Discuss how you would use *out of* with the words in the box.

| danger | condition | touch | reach | sorts | the question |

4   Look at how these expressions are used in the sentences below and opposite. Try to work out what they mean.

a. After the car accident we all thought she was going to die, but she is recovering and is now *out of danger*.
b. I haven't taken any exercise for a long time, so I'm probably *out of condition*.

c. I haven't read any medical books or articles on the subject for a long time, so I'm *out of touch* with recent developments.

d. You must always put pills and medicines somewhere *out of reach*, such as on a high shelf, so that children can't get hold of them. They might think they are sweets and eat them.

e. I'd like to go to the party, but I'm feeling *out of sorts*. I think it's better if I go to bed with a hot water bottle.

f. At the moment, an operation on his leg is *out of the question*. It is far too dangerous and probably wouldn't be a success anyway.

5   Now think of your own sentences, using the expressions above.

How multi-word verbs work
down

*I think you should try to **cut down** (on) the amount you smoke.*

The particle *down* can be used with some verbs to give the idea of reducing something (decreasing in strength, size, or intensity):

*The radio is very loud. Can you **turn** it **down**, please?*

6   Work with your partner. Say what you think the following multi-word verbs mean and give examples of when you would use them.

slow down	bring something down	calm down	die down
cool down	quieten down		

7   In the following sentences, the multi-word verbs are all mixed up. Correct them.

a. This soup is too hot to eat. I'll wait for it to *slow down*.

b. The government is trying to *calm down* the rate of inflation.

c. You are driving too fast. Please *quieten down*.

d. Don't get so angry! Just *bring down*.

e. Can you ask the children to *die down*? They are making so much noise I can't hear myself think!

f. The wind blew strongly for several hours but then it started to *cool down*.

What's the answer?

1 What is the difference between:

a. *to pick up* a disease and *to go down with* a disease?

b. *to wake up* and *to come round*?

c. *to be worn out* and *to be run down*?

2 What is the opposite of *to pass out*?

Jokes

> – Doctor, can you help me out?
> – Certainly. Which way did you come in?
>
> – Doctor, I snore so loudly that I keep myself awake. What can I do?
> – Sleep in another room.
>
> – Doctor, I'm having trouble with my breathing.
> – We'll soon put a stop to that.
>
> – Doctor, I keep seeing double.
> – Sit on the couch, please.
> – Which one?

Speaking and writing

1 Work with your partner. Practise telling the story of Mr Brown. Use multi-word verbs and expressions from this unit.

2 Now write the story of Mr Brown. Use the following multi-word verbs and expressions.

out of condition	to be/go on a diet
to put on (an amount of something)	to give something up
to get through (an amount of something)	out of breath
to cut something out	to knock someone down
to cut down (on) (something)	to come round
to take something up	out of danger

4 A place of your own

Preparation

Work in pairs. Discuss the following question.

– What are the advantages and disadvantages of living away from home when you are a student?

Presentation

1 Tony is a student. He has recently moved into his own flat. He wrote to his friend Paul to tell him about it. When you have read Tony's letter, answer the questions below.

Dear Paul,

I've done it! I've got a place of my own at last! I found it through an agency a couple of weeks ago. I was looking through the paper, when I came across an advertisement for flats, so I gave the agency a ring and went to see what they had. I saw several good flats, but I couldn't make up my mind about them. Then I saw one I really liked. I was in two minds about taking it because the rent was rather high, but I thought it was time I became more independent of my parents, and I'm sure I was getting on their nerves – they said they couldn't put up with the noise from my stereo system any longer! So I moved out and here I am in my own flat!

It's in the suburbs on the outskirts of London, and it's very convenient for the shops. It's on the second floor and consists of a bedroom, a living room, a kitchen, and a bathroom. It's nothing out of the ordinary, but it's in quite good condition.

I moved in last week and I've already put up some shelves and new wallpaper in the living room. At present the kitchen is painted dark brown and has a small window, so it needs brightening up. I haven't finished doing up the bedroom yet. I'm going to convert it into a study and paint it blue so that it will go with the curtains my mother has promised to give me. There's a lovely view from the window – it looks out onto the garden, which I share with four other people.

I get on well with the people living above me, but unfortunately I'm not on good terms with the landlord at the moment. We had an argument about sticking pictures on the wall – he said it would damage the wallpaper. And the people below me say they are fed up with the noise from my stereo!

The good thing is that I've got somewhere I can call my own. I can easily put you up any time you're in London. So don't hesitate – you can drop in any time.

All the best,

Tony.

PS I'm thinking of having a house-warming party at the end of the month, so if you'd like to come, drop me a line or give me a call.

a. How did Tony find the flat?
b. Why did he decide to take it?
c. What are his plans for the flat?
d. What offer does he make?
e. What invitation does he make?

2 Now underline the multi-word verbs in the letter and try to work out what they mean.

Checking understanding

Match the verbs in A with the definitions in B.

A	B
1 to look through something	a. to give someone accommodation
2 to come across someone/something	b. to have a view of somewhere
3 to put up with someone/something	c. to visit someone informally, to pay a casual visit
4 to move out (of somewhere)	d. to match or suit, to make a good combination (for example, of colours)
5 to brighten something up	e. to read something quickly and briefly
6 to look (out) onto something	f. to find something or meet someone by chance
7 to go with something	g. to leave accommodation and take everything with you, to vacate a house or flat
8 to put someone up	h. to make something brighter, less dull, and more full of light
9 to drop in (on someone)	i. to tolerate something, to accept something unpleasant or difficult without complaining

Drills

T.4

Listen and respond to the prompts.

Practice

1   Fill in the gaps below.

I live _____ (a) my own _____ (b) the suburbs _____ (c) the outskirts of London. My flat is _____ (d) the second floor and it's _____ (e) good condition. It consists _____ (f) four rooms and is very convenient _____ (g) the shops. The bedroom looks out onto a garden, which I share _____ (h) four other people. I want to convert the bedroom _____ (i) a study. I found the flat _____ (j) an agency.

Idiomatic expressions

2 Complete the following sentences so that they illustrate the meaning of the idiomatic expressions in Tony's letter.

Example
I thought the play was nothing out of the ordinary, but my friends thought it was great.

a. He really gets on my nerves. He is always . . .
b. I'm not on good terms with the people who live next door . . .
c. I'm fed up with my job because . . .
d. She was in two minds about accepting the job in America because . . .
e. She couldn't make up her mind about the party. On the one hand . . .

3 Work in pairs. Ask your partner to describe where he or she lives. Try to use multi-word verbs, particles, and idiomatic expressions in your questions and answers.

How multi-word verbs work
up

4 The particle *up* can be used with some verbs to give the idea of improving something:

*I haven't finished **doing up** the bedroom yet.*

Look at the sentences and say what you think the verbs in italics mean.

a. I'm going to work in Paris next year, so I really need to *brush up* my French. I studied it at school several years ago but I think I've forgotten a lot of it.
b. Her job is to *train up* people to become clerks or accountants.
c. He didn't know very much about computers, so he decided to *read up on* the subject in preparation for his job interview.
d. He was told that if he wanted to continue working for the company he would have to *smarten up* his appearance.
e. She managed to *build up* the reputation of the company in a very short time.

What's the answer?

1 What is the difference between *to put someone up* and *to put something up?*
2 All the multi-word verbs below are connected in some way. What is the connection?

drop in (on someone) drop by drop round drop over
call in (on someone) call by call round call over call (on someone)

Jokes

> – Some people say you are indecisive. Do you think you have difficulty in making up your mind?
> – Well, yes and no.

> You asked me to drop you a line, so here it is:
> _____ ✎

Speaking and writing

1 Look at the picture story with your partner. Practise telling the story before you write it. You can decide what happens in picture 12. How do you think the story ends?

2 Do you like the story? Why? How much truth is there in it?

3 Now write the story. Try to use some of the following multi-word verbs and expressions.

to be fed up with	to be in two minds	to do up
to put up with	to think over	to see to
to look out onto	to make up one's mind	to throw out
to get on someone's nerves	to move out/in	to put up
to look through		to put in
to come across		

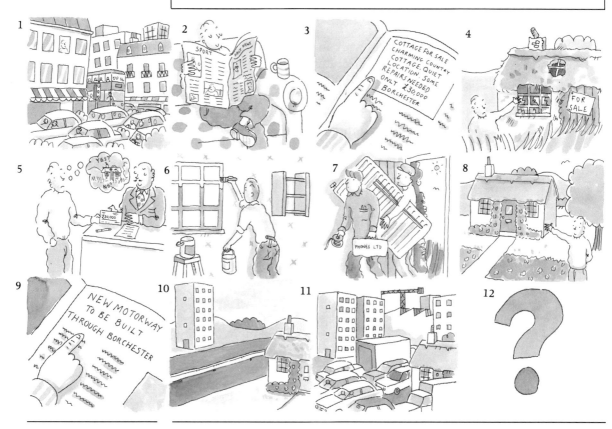

5 Getting away from it all

Preparation

Work in pairs. Discuss the following questions.

– What is your idea of an ideal holiday?
– How important are holidays to you?

Presentation

T.5a

1 You are going to hear four people talking about their last holiday and the importance of holidays in their lives. Make notes in the grid below.

	Last holiday	Importance of holidays
Jean		
Andy		
Susan		
Sheila		

◀ T.5a

2   Listen again to check your answers.

**Checking
understanding**

T.5b

Listen to the sentences with the multi-word verbs in A. Then match the
verbs in A with the definitions in B.

A	B
1 to take off	a. to leave a hotel after paying the bill
2 to pick someone up	b. to break one's journey for a short time
3 to drop someone off	c. to leave the ground and begin flying
4 to get away	d. to walk round a place in order to see what it is like
5 to check out	e. to have a holiday
6 to set off	f. to drive someone where they want to go and leave them there
7 to get back	g. to begin a journey
8 to touch down	h. to collect someone by car or coach, to stop and give someone a lift
9 to look round (somewhere)	i. to land after a flight
10 to stop off	j. to arrive back at the place you started from

Drills

T.5c

Listen and respond to the prompts.

Practice

1   You are on holiday in Rhodes. Your travel representative leaves you a
note giving details of an excursion to the nearby island of Symi. Fill in
the missing words opposite.

Trip to the island of Symi

Hi there!

The arrangements for tomorrow's trip to the island of Symi are as follows:

The coach will _____ us _____(a) at 7.00 a.m. outside the post office – so remember to set your alarm clock! It will take us to Rhodes harbour and then we'll catch the ferry to the island of Symi. When we get there, another coach will _____ us _____ (b) and take us to the main town. We will have about two hours to _____ (c) the shops and have lunch.

At 3.00 p.m. we'll _____ (d) for the village of Pixos. At 5.00 we'll catch the ferry again and we'll _____ (e) to Rhodes harbour at about 7.00. Another coach will _____ us _____ (f) and we'll _____ (g) somewhere for a meal on the way back.

The coach will _____ us _____ (h) at the post office around 10.00, so you'll probably _____ (i) to your apartment about 10.15.

See you tomorrow,

Sharon

2   Work in pairs. Ask and answer questions about the holiday below.

Student A

You have booked a holiday in Lindos on the island of Rhodes. Phone up the travel agent and check the travel details. Use the multi-word verbs below.

take off	get to
drop off	stop off
pick up	check in/out
get back	

Student B

You work in a travel agency. A customer rings up to check his/her travel details. Use the information and the multi-word verbs below.

take off	stop off
pick up	drop off
look round	touch down
check in/out	get back

Island: Rhodes / Holiday resort:
Lindos

1 *what time plane depart?*

2 *direct flight to Rhodes?*

3 *when arrive Rhodes?*

4 *journey to hotel?*

5 *hotel booking arrangements?*

6 *return journey details?*

7 *when collect tickets?*

ISLAND: RHODES   HOLIDAY RESORT: LINDOS

Note time difference = two hours.

Journey details
Flight departs Heathrow Saturday 08.00.
Plane arrives in Athens at 13.00. It stops on the way for 24 hours (sightseeing time).
Plane departs again on Sunday at 16.00.
Plane lands in Rhodes at 16.45.
Passengers collected by coach at 17.15.
Coach leaves them at hotel in Lindos at 18.30.
Must register at hotel before 21.00.

Return journey details
Must leave hotel by 11.00.
Coach collects passengers at 12.00.
Plane leaves 16.00.
Plane lands Heathrow 17.30.
Office open: Monday – Saturday 9.00–6.00.

◄ T.5a

3 Fill in the gaps below. Then listen to Sheila again to check your answers.

a. to look forward _____ doing something

b. to suffer _____ something

c. to complain _____ something _____ someone

d. to insist _____ something

e. to succeed _____ something

f. to be disappointed _____ something

g. to be (dis)satisfied _____ something

h. to be angry _____ something/_____ someone

Idiomatic expressions

4 What do you think the following expressions mean?
How would you say the same thing in your own language?

1 It's just a stone's throw away.
2 Travel broadens the mind.
3 to get away from it all

How multi-word verbs work
Type 1 multi-word verbs are intransitive (they do not take an object).
*We **set off** very early in the morning.*

Type 3 multi-word verbs are transitive (they take an object).
*Can I **look through** your newspaper?*

5 Decide if the multi-word verbs below are Type 1 (intransitive) or Type 3 (transitive).

a. It took him a long time to *get over* his cold. _____

b. Your tie doesn't *go with* your shirt. _____

c. The plane *touched down* without any problems. _____

d. What time will you *get back* tonight? _____

e. Can you *see to* the radio? It isn't working. _____

f. Shall we *stop off* and see Paul on our way home? _____

g. He *came round* two hours after the operation. _____

h. It's good to *get away* at least once a year. _____

i. She *passed out* when she heard the news. _____

j. Did you *come across* anything interesting in the newspaper? _____

back

The particle *back* is often used with verbs to give the meaning of *someone or something returning to the place where he/she/it was before.*

*What time will you **be back** tonight?*

It can also be used to give the idea of reciprocating an action, that is, repeating a similar action.

*I've received a letter inviting us to a party. Shall I **write back** and accept the invitation?*

6 Work with your partner. Look at the verbs below and think of sentences to illustrate what they mean. Say if the verbs have the idea of *returning* or *repeating a similar action* (reciprocating).

ring/phone/call someone back	give something back	walk back
put something back	drive (someone) back	shout back
pay something back	take something back	fly back
play something back	send something back	turn back

What's the answer?

1 What is the opposite of the following?

to check out of a hotel _____   to pick someone up _____

to take off _____   to set off for somewhere _____

2 What is the difference between *When do you go back?* and *When do you get back?*

3 What is the difference between *to get back* and *to turn back?*

Jokes

Come to British Airways!
Breakfast in London!
Lunch in New York!   Luggage in Nairobi!

(Graffiti on a poster advertising British Airways)

WE SEND YOUR LUGGAGE EVERYWHERE

(A badly translated sign above a check-in desk at an airport)

Writing

Write a description of the worst holiday you have ever had. Include details about the journey and the accommodation. Remember to use some of the multi-word verbs and idiomatic expressions from this unit.

6 Family relationships

Preparation

Work in pairs. Discuss the following questions.

– In what ways are you similar to or different from other people in your family?
– Do you think parents should be strict or easy-going?

Presentation

T.6a

Read and/or listen to the following three interviews and answer the questions.

1 What kind of relationship do the children have with their parents?
2 Are the parents strict?
3 According to the mother, what is it like being a parent and what is a good parent?

Interview with 16-year-old daughter Helen

Interviewer How do you get on with your parents?
Helen I think I get on with them very well, really. We don't always see eye to eye on some things, like boyfriends – they don't always approve of them – but on the whole they're very understanding. If I had a personal problem, I think I could confide in them, and if I was ever in trouble I know I could rely on them to help me.
Interviewer How strict are your parents?
Helen Well, my Dad's quite strict about staying out late at night, but I can usually get round him. If I'm nice to him, he lets me come home a bit later. My Mum's always telling me to tidy up my bedroom and put things away after I use them, and I have to do some of the housework. But if I compare them with other parents I know, they aren't very strict.
Interviewer And who are you most like in your family?
Helen Oh, I think I take after my mother. Everybody says we're both very independent and strong-willed. I like to have my own way a lot of the time, but I'm not spoilt. I don't always get my own way. And my parents always tell me off if I do anything wrong.

Interview with 17-year-old son David

Interviewer How do you get on with your parents?
David I look up to them because I know they've worked hard to bring us up properly.
Interviewer How strict are your parents?
David They can be very strict at times. I told my Dad I wanted a

motorbike, but he said it was out of the question – it was too dangerous. My mother is strict about keeping things tidy. I can't get out of doing the washing up and things like that, unless I'm very busy.
Interviewer How do you get on with your sister?
David I never agree with what she says, so we are always arguing. We've never been very close, but I get on all right with her. I think I'm much closer to my mother.

Interview with mother

Interviewer What's it like being a parent?
Mother Bringing up children is very difficult. You always worry about them. You have to be very patient and put up with a lot – like noise and even criticism. And you can't always get through to them – sometimes they just won't listen. But the advantages of being a parent outweigh the disadvantages. The main thing is to enjoy your children while they are young because they grow up so quickly nowadays.
Interviewer How strict are you with your children?
Mother I suppose I'm reasonably strict. They can't do what they like and get away with it, and I tell them off when they do something wrong.
Interviewer And what is the secret of being a good parent?
Mother I think you have to give them confidence and let them know you love them. And you have to set a good example through your own behaviour, otherwise they won't look up to you.
Interviewer And what do you want for your children in the future?
Mother I want them to be happy, and I want them to look back on their childhood as a very happy time in their lives.

Checking understanding

Work in pairs. Try to work out from the context the meaning of the multi-word verbs in *italics* in the passage. Then match the verbs in A with the definitions in B.

A	B
1 to get round someone	a. to respect and admire someone, to have a very good opinion of someone
2 to take after someone	b. to escape being punished for something
3 to tell someone off (for doing something)	c. to think about something that happened in the past
4 to look up to someone	d. to reprimand, to speak severely to someone because they have done something wrong.
5 to bring someone up	e. to persuade someone to let you do or have something, usually by flattering them
6 to get out of doing something	f. to raise a child, to look after a child until it is adult and try to give it particular beliefs and attitudes
7 to get through to someone	g. to resemble a member of your family in appearance or character
8 to grow up	h. to avoid having to do something
9 to get away with something	i. to succeed in making someone understand the meaning of what one is saying
10 to look back (on something)	j. to become more adult and mature

Drills

T.6b

Listen and respond to the prompts.

Practice

1 Fill in the gaps below.

a. to dis/approve _____ someone/something

b. to confide _____ someone

c. to rely _____ someone

d. to compare someone/something _____ someone/something

e. to (dis)agree _____ someone/something

f. to argue _____ someone _____ something

g. to worry _____ someone/something

h. to listen _____ someone/something

Idiomatic expressions

2 What do you think the following expressions mean?

1 to see eye to eye (with someone) (on something)
2 to have/get one's own way
3 to be close to someone
4 to be the black sheep of the family
5 to take someone's side

Now decide which expressions you could use in the sentences below.

a. The problem is that her parents never stop her doing anything that she wants to do. She's become a very spoilt child as a result.
b. My family is very ashamed of my brother and never talk about him. He was expelled from school and has been in prison twice.
c. Whenever I had an argument with my mother or father, I could always rely on my grandparents to support me.
d. My father and I usually agree about most things, but when it comes to politics we have completely different views.
e. I can talk to my sister about my problems because I know she will understand me and share my feelings.

3 Work with your partner. Take turns asking and answering the questions opposite. Try to use the multi-word verbs and expressions in the box in your answers, as well as the verbs above.

Example
A *How do you get on with the other people in your family?*
B *I don't get on with my sisters very well, but I'm very close to my mother. I feel I can confide in her.*

bring up	look back on	tell off
get on with	look up to	take after
get away with	grow up	get round
have one's own way	see eye to eye	be close to

a. What kind of relationship do you have with the people in your family?
b. Are you similar to anyone in your family?
c. Do you have the same opinions as other members of your family?
d. Where did you spend your childhood?
e. Who took care of you when you were very young?
f. Did you have a strict upbringing?
g. When were you reprimanded as a child/teenager?
h. Were you able to do what you wanted all the time?
i. Who did you admire and respect when you were a child/teenager?
j. When you think about the past, what do you remember?

4   Work with a different partner. Use the multi-word verbs and idiomatic expressions you have learnt to describe your relationship with one of the following people.

grandparent	teacher	uncle/aunt	parent
brother/sister	neighbour	boss	cousin

How multi-word verbs work

5   Match a sentence in A with one in B, and mark the stress. Then practise saying the questions and answers. The first one has been done for you.

A	B
1 Do you respect your parents?	a. No, he got away with it.
2 Do you like David?	b. No, I can't get through to him.
3 Did he do the washing up?	c. No, he puts up with it.
4 Does he listen to you?	d. No, he got out of it.
5 Was he punished for the crime?	e. No, I must get down to it.
6 Have you done the homework?	f. No, I don't get on with him.
7 Has he complained about the noise?	g. Yes, I look up to them.

What is the stress rule for multi-word verbs that have two particles?

What's the answer?

1 What is the difference between *to grow up* and *to bring someone up*?

2 What is the opposite of *to look up to someone*?

3 What is the noun of a. and adjective of b?

  a. to bring up (→ noun)   She had a very strict _____ .
  b. to grow up (→ adjective) He doesn't behave in a very _____ way.

Jokes

Mother Tell your boyfriend he must bring you back here by ten o'clock tonight – and not a minute later!
Daughter Oh, mother! I'm not a child any longer.
Mother I know. That's why I want you back here by ten.

Pupil Sir, can you be told off for something you haven't done?
Teacher Of course not.
Pupil Oh, that's good, because I haven't done my homework.

One day a boy came home from school and his mother heard him use a very bad word. She was very angry.

'Where did you learn that word?' she asked.
'From Chaucer,' he replied.
'Well, don't play with Chaucer any more,' she said.

(Note: Chaucer was a famous medieval writer.)

Speaking

Work in pairs. Discuss *one* of the following questions.

– Should boys and girls be brought up in exactly the same way?
– What are the advantages and disadvantages of being an only child?

Writing

Using the multi-word verbs and idiomatic expressions you have learnt in this unit, write about a relationship which has had an important influence on you.

You are what you wear

Preparation

How important are clothes to you?
Look at the picture below. Describe what you think is happening and why.

Presentation

T.7a

Listen to the story of the Emperor's new clothes. Make a note of the multi-word verbs that are used and what you think they mean. Then discuss the questions below with a partner.

a. Why did the Emperor want the two men to make the clothes?
b. Why did the Emperor send his old and honest minister to see the two men?
c. Why did one of the two men ask the Emperor to try on the invisible clothes?
d. Why didn't anyone say the Emperor was wearing nothing?
e. Why did the Emperor go through with the procession?
f. Why was the little boy the first person to say 'The Emperor has nothing on'?
g. Why did the Emperor carry on with the procession?
h. What do you think the story is trying to say?

Checking understanding

Look at how the multi-word verbs are used in the listening text on page 81. Then match the verbs in A with the definitions in B.

A	B
1 to take something off	a. to dress oneself in clothes or jewellery
2 to have (got) (something) on	b. to put on a piece of clothing to see if it fits and looks nice
3 to try something on	c. to do something difficult or unpleasant
4 to carry on (with something)	d. to fasten something (a button or a zip)
5 to go through with something	e. to continue with something, in spite of difficulties or interruptions
6 to wear out	f. to be wearing a piece of clothing
7 to dress up	g. to remove clothes, to undress
8 to put something on	h. to put on clothes without difficulty because they aren't too small
9 to do something up	i. to wear smart clothes for a special occasion
10 to get into something	j. to become useless because it has been used so often

Drills

T.7b

Listen and respond to the prompts.

Practice

1   Fill in the gaps opposite.

Tim is seventeen and at the moment he doesn't care very much _____ (a) anything except clothes. He's only interested _____ (b) what is _____ (c) fashion. He spends most of his money _____ (d) brightly coloured shirts and tight trousers. He is very proud_____ (e) them and most people comment _____ (f) them when they see him. He has no difficulty _____ (g) finding the clothes he wants because he works in a boutique. He thinks he has very good taste in clothes, but his mother thinks he looks awful. 'It's all a question of taste,' he says, 'and there's no arguing about tastes, is there?'

2 Work with a partner. Take turns telling one another the story of the Emperor's clothes. The following prompts may help.

- the Emperor
- the two dishonest men
- the magical clothes
- making the clothes
- the Emperor sends his minister

- the minister's visit
- the Emperor's visit
- the Emperor tries on the clothes
- the procession
- the little boy

T.7c

3 Listen to four situations in which people are talking about clothes. Decide what the situation is and who is talking.

4 Put the following expressions in the sentences below.

out of fashion   out of luck   out of this world   out of stock
out of date

a. I'm sorry, madam, we don't have any of these jumpers in size 14. We're completely _____ . I don't think we'll be getting any more of them till next year.
b. I'm afraid you're _____ , sir. We've sold all the tickets for the plays you would like to see.
c. It was the best play I've ever seen. The production was absolutely fantastic. It was _____ .
d. I can't use this passport any more. It's _____ . I'll have to get a new one.
e. He doesn't worry about his appearance or what is in fashion. He always wears clothes that are _____ .

Idiomatic expressions

5 Look at the expressions below. Which ones are similar in meaning? How would you express the same idea in your own language?

1 A wolf in sheep's clothing.
2 There's no arguing about tastes.
3 Beauty is only skin deep.

4 You can't go by appearances.
5 One man's meat is another man's poison.
6 Beauty is in the eye of the beholder.

Which of the above expressions could you use in the following situations?

a. You think a piece of modern sculpture is ugly but your friend thinks it's beautiful.
b. Your sister is in love with a man who seems very nice and friendly, but you think that underneath he's a horrible, selfish person who only wants her money.
c. You meet someone who gives the impression of being very poor. You find out later that in fact this person is very rich.
d. You meet an attractive looking person who seems very nice, but you later find out this person is unkind and unfriendly.

How multi-word verbs work

up

The particle *up* can be used with some verbs to give the idea of completion:

*We'd better **drink up**. The bar closes in five minutes.*

In this sentence, *drink up* = finish drinking. Several verbs use *up* in this way.

eat up	tidy up	wash up	dry up	clean up	clear up

6 Use the multi-word verbs above to correct the following sentences.

a. Look at all these dirty dishes. I really don't feel like doing them. Could you eat them up?
b. My room looks like a bomb hit it. I can't find anything. I must dry it up.
c. 'Tidy up all your vegetables or you won't grow big and strong,' my mother used to tell me.
d. After the party her friends offered to help her wash up the mess.
e. I'll wash the dishes if you clean them up.

What's the answer?

1 Write down the opposite of the following.

   – out of fashion _____   – out of stock _____

   – out of date _____   – to take something off _____

   – out of luck _____   – to do something up _____

2 What is the difference between *to go through with something* and *to carry on with something?*

3 What is the difference between *to take off* and *to take something off?*

Jokes

> *Man in clothes shop* Can I try on that suit in the window?
> *Shop assistant* No sir, you'll have to use the changing-room like everyone else.
>
> *Interviewer* Is it true you had nothing on when those photos were taken?
> *Film star* Oh, no. I had the radio on.

Writing

Write the story of *Cinderella*. Here are some notes to help you.

– Cinderella's mother dies. Her father decides to marry again.
– Her stepmother is cruel and her stepsisters are ugly and horrible.
– She is treated badly and has to do all the housework.
– Her clothes become very poor and old.
– Everyone is invited to attend a ball at the palace.
– The two stepsisters discuss what to wear. They can't decide. Cinderella helps them.
– Cinderella can't go to the ball. She has nothing to wear.
– Her fairy godmother appears and arranges for her to go to the ball.
– Her dress is very beautiful. She must return before midnight.
– She dances with the prince. He falls in love with her.
– At 12 o'clock Cinderella leaves quickly, leaving behind a glass shoe.
– The prince decides to marry the person who can wear the shoe.
– The shoe is too small for the two ugly sisters.
– The shoe fits Cinderella. She marries the prince.

Begin the story *Once upon a time . . .* Write it in the past tense and end the story with *. . . and they lived happily ever after.* Try to include the multi-word verbs and idiomatic expressions in the box.

to make up one's mind	to dress up	in/out of fashion
to tidy up	to put something on	to go with something
to clean up	to take something off	out of this world
to wear out	to try something on	to get into something

8 A narrow escape

Preparation

Think about the question below.

– Have you ever been in a frightening situation?

Tell the class what happened.

Presentation

Read the text below and find the answers to the questions.

1 What is known about how the fire started?
2 How did the residents escape the fire?

Hotel blaze escape drama

A blaze swept through a hotel in London yesterday, leaving damage estimated at £200,000. Some of the residents staying in the hotel at the time were able to escape via the roof onto adjoining premises.

At present it is not known how the fire started. It seems the fire *broke out* in the early hours of the morning. The fire alarm *went off* at around 2.00 a.m. It is thought it was *set off* by smoke coming from one of the bedrooms on the first floor. The fire spread quickly from the first floor to the second floor. The fire-brigade were *called in* immediately, and firefighters were on the scene within fifteen minutes, but by this time the hotel was already in flames. They fought the blaze and managed to get it under control, though it took them two hours to *put* the fire *out*.

Senior Fire Officer Mike Jones, who was in charge of the operation, said, 'It's a miracle no one was hurt. We had to break down several doors to rescue some of the residents from their rooms. Our people did a wonderful job. Two of them are suffering from smoke inhalation, but it doesn't look too serious at the moment.'

Mrs Lunnon, a resident, said, 'I never want to *go through* an experience like that again. Everywhere was on fire. I'm just so relieved the firefighters succeeded in getting to us so quickly. Without their help we wouldn't have *got out*.'

Another resident, Mr Dale, said, 'I heard the alarm *go off* and then people started screaming. It was very frightening. My wife and I had a narrow escape. We managed to *get out* of the building just in time – as we left the third floor it burst into flames! We could hear people *calling out* for help, but we couldn't do anything to help them.'

The hotel manager said, 'The fire probably started by accident. Perhaps someone was smoking in bed, forgot to *put out* their cigarette, and accidentally set fire to the bedclothes. Some people are very careless, and things can catch fire very easily.'

A policeman said, 'We will be *looking into* the causes of the fire. We think it started by accident, though at this stage we don't want to *rule* anything *out*.'

Checking understanding

Look at the text and try to work out from the context the meaning of the multi-word verbs in *italics*. Then match the verbs in A with the definitions in B.

A	B
1 to break out	a. to cause something to start working or happening
2 to go off	b. to experience or suffer something unpleasant
3 to set something off	c. to begin suddenly, usually something unpleasant
4 to call someone in/out	d. to leave, to escape
5 to put something out	e. to exclude something, to decide something is impossible
6 to go through something	f. to shout loudly in order to attract someone's attention
7 to get out (of somewhere)	g. to extinguish something, to stop something burning
8 to call out	h. to ask someone professional to come and provide help
9 to look into something	i. to operate, making a sudden loud noise
10 to rule something out	j. to investigate something

Drills

T.8

Listen and respond to the prompts.

Practice

1 Fill in the gaps below. Then check your answers with the text of the hotel blaze escape.

SENIOR FIRE OFFICER'S REPORT

We received an emergency call at 2.15 a.m. which said the Grove Hotel was _____ (a) fire. We were _____ (b) the scene within fifteen minutes. The first and second floors of the hotel were _____ (c) flames when we arrived. But we succeeded _____ (d) getting the fire _____ (e) control after two hours. I was _____ (f) charge of the whole operation. Two of our people are still in hospital suffering _____ (g) the effects of smoke inhalation.

At the moment it appears that the fire started _____ (h) accident, but it is not clear why the fire spread so quickly or why the third floor burst _____ (i) flames.

Idiomatic expressions

2 Look at the following idiomatic expressions and say what you think they mean.

*I **had a narrow escape** this morning. I was cycling to work when a lorry knocked me off my bike. The driver stopped and got out to see if I was all right. He was **as white as a sheet** and I was **shaking like a leaf**. Fortunately I had landed on some grass and wasn't hurt.*

Have you ever had a narrow escape? If yes, describe what happened.

3 Work with your partner. Describe what is happening in the pictures below and say what you think will or might happen next. Use the multi-word verbs, idiomatic expressions, and prepositions in this unit.

a.

Comment on the smoke detector, the curtains, what you think the woman will do, what might happen next.

b.

Comment on the cigarette, the bedclothes, the hotel fire alarm, what might happen next.

c.

Comment on the man in the car, the petrol on the road, what might happen next.

4 Work with your partner. Write a brief news item for the two pictures below. Read it out to the rest of the class.

1

2

burst into

5 *It burst into flames* means 'It suddenly started burning'.

To burst into is often used to describe changing emotional states. How would you say the following?

He suddenly started crying. _____

She suddenly started laughing. _____

He suddenly started singing. _____

The audience suddenly began to
applaud. _____

Give a situation where each of these things might happen.

How multi-word verbs work

6 Decide if the following multi-word verbs are Type 1, 2, or 3.

a. The fire alarm went off at 2.00 a.m. _____

b. He set off the fire alarm. _____

c. They called in the fire brigade. _____

d. People were calling out for help. _____

e. They put out the fire very quickly. _____

f. We went through a terrible experience. _____

g. Fortunately everyone got out safely. _____

h. A fire has broken out on the first floor. _____

i. We must look into this very carefully. _____

j. We can't rule out the possibility
that the fire was started deliberately. _____

out

7 1 The particle *out* can be combined with verbs to indicate *movement from somewhere inside to somewhere outside* (*to get out, to check out of somewhere, to go out*), or to a *location outside the home* (*to move out*).

Say what you think the following multi-word verbs mean, and give examples of when you would use them.

to eat out	to invite someone out	to camp out
to stay out	to take someone out	

2 The particle *out* can also be used with verbs to give the idea of excluding something (*to rule something out, to cut something out*).

Say what you think the following multi-word verbs mean and give examples of when you would use them.

to leave someone/something out	to keep someone/something out
to shut someone/something out	

What's the answer?

1 What is the opposite of *by accident?*
2 What is the opposite of *under control?*
3 What is the difference between *to be in control* and *to be under control?*
   e.g. 'The situation is under control' and 'The police are in control of the situation'.
4 What is the difference between *to go off* and *to set something off?*
5 What is the difference between *to set off* and *to set something off?*

Jokes

A hole has appeared in Westminster Road. The police are looking into it.
(From a newspaper report)

'Can you put the cat out?'
'Why? Is it on fire?'

Writing

Write a story called 'A narrow escape'. Try to use the multi-word verbs, expressions, and particles from this unit.

9 Getting on in life

Preparation

Work in pairs. Discuss the following questions.

- What is your idea of a good job?
- Have you ever had a job you didn't like? What happened?

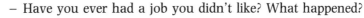

Presentation

T.9a

Listen to two people, Jeremy and Angela, describing how they came to choose their careers. Make notes while you listen. Then work with your partner. Decide if the following statements are true (T) or false (F) and explain why.

a. ☐ Jeremy was made unemployed because the company wanted to save money.

b. ☐ The company went out of business because of the poor economic climate.

c. ☐ Jeremy was offered several jobs in other similar companies but he rejected them.

d. ☐ Jeremy's application to a small magazine was successful.

e. ☐ Angela's father wanted her to be ambitious.

f. ☐ She needed special training to do her job as a secretary.

g. ☐ She had to spend a lot of time doing her job.

h. ☐ She couldn't live on her salary.

i. ☐ A few things about her job depressed her.

j. ☐ She chose law as her career.

Checking understanding

Look at the listening text on page 83 and try to work out the meaning of the multi-word verbs from the context. Then match the verbs in A with the definitions in B.

A	B
1 to cut back (on) (something)	a. to learn something without difficulty or special study
2 to close (something) down	b. to make someone feel depressed
3 to turn someone/something down	c. to close something (a factory or organization) temporarily or permanently
4 to take someone on	d. to manage to survive and have a satisfactory life
5 to get on	e. to use or require a certain amount of time, effort, or space
6 to pick something up	f. to employ someone
7 to take up an amount of something	g. to choose something as one's career
8 to get by (on something)	h. to refuse or reject someone/something
9 to get someone down	i. to reduce something, especially to save money
10 to go in for something	j. to succeed, to be successful in one's job

Drills

T.9b

Listen and respond to the prompts.

Practice

1 Fill in the gaps below. The last one is the name of a profession.

Originally I worked _____ (a) a school teacher, but I applied _____ (b) a grant to study medicine at university and was accepted _____ (c) the course. I specialized _____ (d) mental disorders, and then started my present job. I believe completely _____ (e) what I am doing, I never take any time _____ (f) work, and I am totally committed _____ (g) my clients. I have to listen very carefully _____ (h) what they say, and I sometimes explain _____ (i) them what I think the problem is. Sometimes they start to depend _____ (j) me too much. What is my job? Oh, I forgot to tell you. I am a _____ (k).

Idiomatic expressions

2 Look at how the following expressions are used in the listening text. What do you think they mean? How would you say number 4 and 6 in your own language?

1 to get on in life/the world
2 to be cut out for something
3 to refuse (something) point-blank
4 That's the last straw!
5 to make one's way in the world
6 The world is one's oyster.

Use the expressions above to complete the following sentences.

a. After four weeks of working in a school, he realized he wasn't _____ teaching. He didn't have enough patience.
b. Although she worked hard and was ambitious, she didn't _____ . Perhaps she was just unlucky.
c. She was young, intelligent, free, and rich. The world _____ .
d. Sarah's two young children had behaved badly all day, so when they threw their dinner on the floor, she said '_____' and immediately put them to bed.
e. The Director was rather shocked when she refused his offer _____ . He wasn't used to receiving _____ refusals.

3 Work with your partner. Take turns interviewing one another, using the questions below. Try to use the following multi-word verbs and expressions in your questions and answers.

cut out for	go in for	get by	get on (in life/the
take on	turn down	apply for	world)
pick up	take up	get someone down	be accepted onto/for

Example
A *What profession do you think you are **cut out for**?*
B *I think I'm **cut out for** acting because I like speaking in public.*

a. Which of these jobs are you most/least suited to? Why?

☐ business management   ☐ acting
☐ administrative work   ☐ nursing
☐ teaching   ☐ secretarial work
☐ social work   ☐ academic work

b. What made you choose your present career or course of study?
c. What kind of things make you feel depressed at work or at school?
d. What aspects of your work or study require most time?
e. How important is it to be successful in life? Why?
f. How important is it to have a job that pays a lot of money? Why?
g. Have you acquired any new skills recently?
h. Where did you learn them?

T.9c

4 Listen to seven people talking about their work. What are their jobs?

How multi-word verbs work

5 It is possible to say 'We must cut back' without including an object in the sentence. However, if the object is included, we can add another particle:

*We must **cut back on** expenditure.*

With this particular multi-word verb the particle *on* is optional. The same is true of *to cut down (on) (something)*:

*I must **cut down on** the amount of chocolate I eat.*

Here are some more multi-word verbs which can be used with or without an object (they can behave like Type 1 or Type 4):

She's falling behind.	How are you getting on?
She dropped in.	They've moved out.
Shall we carry on?	I never look back.
I get by.	We don't get on.

However, if these verbs take an object, they *always* need another particle. Supply the missing particles in the sentences below.

a. I'm falling behind _____ my work at school.

b. How are you getting on _____ your studies?

c. She dropped in _____ us last weekend.

d. We've moved out _____ our flat.

e. Please carry on _____ what you were saying.

f. I often look back _____ my childhood.

g. I can't get by _____ less than £50 a week.

h. Stephen doesn't get on _____ his maths teacher.

What's the answer?

1 When some shops *close down* they have a sale in order to sell all their remaining goods. What is this sale called?

SALE

2 *To close (something) down* and *to shut (something) down* mean the same thing. What multi-word verbs have the opposite meaning?

3 So far this book has covered over twenty-five multi-word verbs with the particle *up*. Fill in as many as you can in the diagram.

Jokes

Q How much training do you need to do to become a rubbish collector?
A *None. You pick it up as you go along.*

Q How many psychiatrists do you need to change a light bulb?
A *Only one, but the light bulb must really want to change.*

Speaking

Work with your partner. Choose a job and decide how you can describe it without saying what the job is. Try not to 'give the game away' by making it too easy. Read your description to the rest of the class. They must guess what the job is. They can also ask you questions about it.

Speaking and writing

Work with your partner. Look at the picture story and practise telling it. Discuss what multi-word verbs and idiomatic expressions you can use. Then write the story together.

A nightmare journey

Preparation Look at the question below. Tell the class about it.

– What is the worst journey you have ever made? What happened?

Presentation Put the following seven paragraphs in the correct order.

My nightmare journey

a. 'Aren't we going to run out of petrol quite soon?' I said. 'No, don't worry, there's plenty left,' he said. Five minutes later the car came to a standstill. We were out of petrol. Martin told me not to worry and said he was sure there was a petrol station somewhere nearby. He got out of the car and walked off. Much to my surprise, he came back ten minutes later with a can full of petrol. He put the petrol in the tank, got in, and we drove off. I felt more relaxed now, and thought that everything would be all right. Two miles later the car broke down.

b. Martin switched on the windscreen wipers, but we couldn't see the road very well. A few minutes later we couldn't make out anything because the rain was so heavy. I warned him about the dangers of driving on wet roads, but instead of slowing down, he speeded up. He said it was getting late. Fortunately, we finally found the street where my interview was to take place. Martin turned to me and said, 'Better late than never'. As he said this, a car pulled out in front of us without warning. Martin managed to swerve just in time to avoid hitting it – but he ran into a parked car instead. The parked car was beyond repair – it was a complete write-off.

c. The following weekend Martin picked me up at 8.30 a.m. He said his alarm clock hadn't gone off and he had overslept, so we set off later than we had planned. My mother was quite excited by the idea of my going to London for an interview, and she came to the front door to see us off. Unfortunately, it was the rush hour, and we were held up in a traffic jam for the next thirty minutes, but eventually the road was clear and we headed for the motorway. I noticed we were short of petrol and pointed this out to Martin.

d. I didn't panic, but I could feel the nervous tension building up in my stomach. 'Don't worry,' he said, 'I know what's wrong with it. I'll fix it in no time at all.' An hour later he was still under the car trying to repair it – but without success. Then another car pulled up next to us and the driver asked if we needed any help. He asked where we were heading for and, when we told him, he pointed out we were going in the wrong direction. He repaired the car, we thanked him for helping us, and we set off again. I don't know how it happened, but instead of arriving in London we ended up in Manchester.

e. The worst journey I have ever made was the time when I had to go to London for a job interview. I was living in York, in the north of England, at the time and my car was under repair. I planned to go by train, but a friend called Martin said, 'No, don't go by train. You know how unreliable they are. They never run on time. I'm going to London next week, so I can give you a lift.' I told him I had to be at the interview by 3.00 o'clock without fail. He assured me we would arrive in time. 'Don't worry,' he said. 'We'll be there in no time.'

f. Martin got out of the car and told the other driver he was responsible for the accident. The other driver blamed Martin for what had happened. I left them arguing and went in for my interview. I apologized for being five minutes late, but they said it was all right because the interviewer hadn't arrived yet. When he came in, I recognized him – it was the man who had pulled out in front of us. I didn't get the job.

g. Martin told me not to worry. He said he knew a quick route to London from Manchester that would reduce our journey time by half. This sounded too good to be true, but I tried to believe him. He said that if we drove fast, we would make up for lost time. To some extent this was true, because he did drive faster, but unfortunately a police car caught up with us and told us to pull over to the side of the road. The policeman fined him for speeding and we drove off. We continued our journey. We were near London when it started to rain.

Checking understanding

Look at how the following multi-word verbs are used in the text. Then match the verbs in A with the definitions in B.

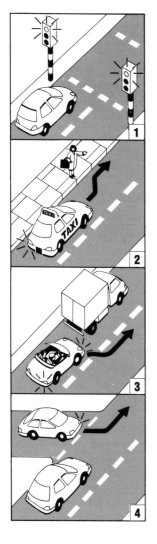

A	B
1 to break down	a. to manage to see or read something
2 to pull over	b. to have no more of something
3 to hold someone/something up	c. to find yourself in a place or situation that you had not intended
4 to pull out	d. to delay someone or something
5 to see someone off	e. to move or travel towards somewhere
6 to end up somewhere	f. to stop working because of mechanical failure (of a vehicle or machine)
7 to pull up	g. to to accompany someone to a place of departure and say goodbye
8 to head for somewhere	h. to slow down and stop a vehicle
9 to run out (of something)	i. to drive a vehicle into a different or faster lane (in order to overtake)
10 to make something out	j. to move a vehicle closer to the side of the road either to stop or to allow other vehicles to pass

Drills

T.10

Listen and respond to the prompts.

Practice

1 Look at the pictures above. Match them with the three multi-word verbs below.

pull over/pull out/pull up

1 _____   2 _____   3 _____   4 _____

2 Fill in the gaps below.

> I remember the day I passed my driving test. My driving instructor complimented me
> _____ (a) my driving skills and congratulated me _____ (b) passing my
> test the first time I took it. It started to rain and he warned me _____ (c) the
> dangers of driving in wet conditions. I thanked him _____ (d) all his help and
> drove off. Then I had an accident. A car pulled out in front of me and I crashed into
> it. The driver of the other car blamed me _____ (e) the accident and refused to
> apologize _____ (f) what had happened although it was completely his fault.

3 Put one word in each of the spaces below and then check your answers with the text.

a. I have to report to the police station on 2 March _____ fail.
b. I can't use my car at the moment. It's in the garage _____ repair.
c. The engineer tried to fix the machine, but _____ success.
d. I asked the mechanic what was wrong _____ my car engine and he said I needed a new one. He said it was so old it was _____ repair.
e. The terrorist bomb exploded _____ warning.

4 Work with a partner and retell the story of the nightmare journey, using the pictures below.

Time expressions

5   Discuss what the following time expressions mean.

The trains never run *on time*.
He assured me we would arrive *in time* for the interview.
He swerved *just in time* to avoid hitting the car.
I'll fix it *in no time at all*.

Now put one time expression in each of the sentences below.

a. The plane wasn't delayed. It took off _____ .
b. We arrived _____ to hear the beginning of the concert.
c. I thought it would take her a long time to complete this exercise, but she finished it _____ .
d. I'm afraid we weren't _____ to save him.
e. The bomb exploded immediately after we left the building – we left _____ .

Idiomatic expressions

6   Discuss what the following expressions mean, and think of situations when you would use them.

1 to make up for lost time
2 My patience is running out.
3 I'll keep my fingers crossed for you.
4 Better late than never.
5 It's better to be safe than sorry.

How multi-word verbs work
up
*Instead of slowing down, he decided to **speed up**.*

The particle *up* can be used with some verbs to give the idea of an increase in quantity or intensity:

*We must **hurry up** or we're going to be late.*

7   Complete the following sentences with multi-word verbs that use the particle *up*.

a. I can't hear the radio. Can you _____ , please?
b. The cost of living is _____ all the time.
c. I'm afraid this is a very bad line and I can't hear what you're saying. Can you _____ , please?
d. This soup isn't very hot. Shall I _____ ?
e. You're still very weak after your illness. I think you need to _____ your strength before you go back to work.
f. The airline company was losing money, so it was forced to _____ prices.

off
*The policeman got into his car and **drove off**.*

The particle *off* can be used with some verbs to give the idea of movement away from somewhere:

*He gave me the money for the books but he **walked off** before I could give him his change.*

8 Complete the following sentences with multi-word verbs that use the particle *off*.

a. The plane was meant to leave at 6.00 a.m. but it didn't _____ until 9.00 a.m.
b. At the end of the film the two lovers got into a boat and _____ into the sunset.
c. The small boy took my purse from my bag and _____ before I could catch him.
d. The next morning we _____ on our journey to see the Himalayas.
e. I would like to jump on a plane and _____ to somewhere exotic and warm.
f. He jumped onto his horse and _____ at speed.

What's the answer?

What is the difference between *to be short of something* and *to be out of something?*

Jokes

A traffic policeman noticed that a driver was knitting while driving along. He got on his motorbike, caught up with the driver and shouted, 'Pull over!' The driver shouted back, 'No, a pair of socks'.

Policeman Why were you speeding?
Driver Well, officer, my brakes are so worn out that I wanted to get home before I had an accident.

Writing

Using the multi-word verbs, idiomatic expressions, and prepositions you have learnt in this unit, write a description of the worst journey you have ever made.

What's in the news?

Work in pairs. Discuss the following questions.

- How often do you listen to the news on TV/radio? What does it depend on?
- What news items do you remember from recent weeks? Why?

Presentation

T.11a

Look at the incomplete news headlines below. See if you can predict what they will be about. Then listen to the news headlines. Fill in the missing words and take notes on each of the news items.

1 | Thieves _____ at the Royal Gallery

2 | **Ship _____ at sea near the Sussex Coast**

3 | Three men _____ of Brixton prison

4 | PLANE _____ IN JUNGLE

5 | Chemical factory _____

6 | **SEVERE WEATHER _____ TOWNS IN THE NORTH**

7 | *Damaged plane _____ safely*

Checking understanding

Look at the multi-word verbs in the tapescript on page 86. Then match the verbs in A with the definitions in B. Note that *to pick someone up* occurs twice but with different meanings.

A	B
1 to pick someone up	a. to escape from a place where one is a prisoner
2 to pick someone up	b. to catch or arrest someone
3 to cut out	c. to succeed in stealing something and escaping with it
4 to blow (something) up	d. to be ready to provide help or take action if it is needed
5 to make off	e. to explode, to destroy something with explosives
6 to break into somewhere/to break in	f. to stop working (of an engine or machine)
7 to cut something/someone off	g. to enter a building or room illegally or by force
8 to get away with something	h. to isolate something or someone from something
9 to break out (of somewhere)	i. to rescue someone from danger, especially from the sea
10 to stand by	j. to leave in a hurry, especially to escape from other people

Drills

T.11b

Listen and respond to the prompts.

Practice

1   Fill in the gaps below.

'What's _____ (a) the newspaper today?'

'It says here that crime is _____ (b) the increase, a man has been put

_____ (c) trial for murder, two English passengers were _____ (d) board a

plane that came down in Brazil, and two escaped prisoners are still _____ (e)

the run from the police.'

'Oh, and what's _____ (f) TV tonight?'

2   Here is a news report on two of the men who broke out of prison. Fill in
the gaps below. Then listen to the report and check your answers.

The two men who broke out of Brixton Prison yesterday, John Ross and Steven

Blake, were described as 'dangerous criminals' by the police.

Last year Ross was arrested _____ (a) armed robbery and charged

_____ (b) a variety of crimes, including assault and car theft. A court found him

guilty of all the charges and he was sentenced _____ (c) four years in prison.

Blake was accused _____ (d) robbing a jeweller's shop in Knightsbridge and

causing serious bodily harm, but there was insufficient evidence to convict him

_____ (e) the crime. He was also suspected _____ (f) being involved in a

bank robbery in Hertford. However, he was found guilty of breaking into offices and

stealing over £10,000. He was sentenced _____ (g) three years in prison.

3   Work with your partner. Use the multi-word verbs and prepositions
above to talk about the pictures opposite. Say what you think has
happened, is happening, and might or will happen next. Then choose one
of the pictures and produce a small news item to read aloud to the rest of
the class.

Idiomatic expression

4   *Crime doesn't pay.* What does this expression mean? Do you agree? Why?

Multi-word verbs as nouns and adjectives

Some multi-word verbs can be used to make nouns and adjectives. They are usually made by combining the infinitive of the verb stem with the particle. If your car *broke down* on the motorway you could say:

*I had a **breakdown** on the motorway, so I called the **breakdown** service.*

Similarly, the verb *to get away* (= to escape) can be used to form a noun or an adjective:

*The robbers made their **getaway** in a blue car. The next day the police found the **getaway** car a short distance from the scene of the crime.*

The stress is normally on the first part of the word (**'break**down, **'get**away).

5 Nouns and adjectives that derive from multi-word verbs are sometimes used in newspaper headlines. Complete the ones below.

a. Someone *broke in* and stole several paintings from the Royal Gallery last night.

> _____ AT ROYAL GALLERY

b. Many cars were *held up* for over three hours on the M25 motorway.

> **THREE HOUR** _____ **ON M25**

c. Three prisoners have *broken out* of Brixton Prison.

> _____ **AT BRIXTON PRISON**

d. The government wants to *cut back* on the amount it spends on defence.

> DEFENCE _____ ANNOUNCED

e. Someone has invented a new switch which makes dangerous machines *cut out* if they become too hot. The invention will save many lives.

> NEW _____ SWITCH WILL SAVE LIVES

What's the answer?

1 What is the difference between *to blow up* and *to blow something up*?
2 *To pick someone/something up* can have several meanings. How many can you think of?

Jokes

> A nervous plane passenger heard the following announcement while waiting for his flight:
> 'Will passengers please prepare for their final departure.'
>
> **Nervous plane passenger** *How often do planes of this type crash?*
> **Flight attendant** *Only once.*

Speaking and writing

Look at the picture story with your partner and practise telling it. Discuss what multi-word verbs and expressions you can use. Now write the story.

12 Across a crowded room

Preparation

Work in pairs. Discuss the following questions.

- Do you believe in love at first sight? Why?/Why not?
- What vocabulary do you know for describing the different stages of a relationship (at the beginning you *get to know someone*, etc.)?

Presentation

1 The pictures below are in the wrong order. Discuss them with your partner and think about a possible order. The first one has been done for you.

2 Now read the story and put the pictures in **1** in the correct order. Write the relevant multi-word verbs and idiomatic expressions under each of the pictures. Then discuss their meaning with your partner.

ACROSS A CROWDED ROOM

It was love at first sight. I saw her standing on the other side of a crowded room sipping a glass of wine. Our eyes met. I walked over to her and said, 'You seem to be on your own. Can I join you?'

She smiled and said yes. At first she came across as rather shy, but as I got to know her better I found out she was an open and confident person who was easy to get on with. At the end of the party I said I would like to see her again and asked her out for a meal the following week.

I took her out to a small Italian restaurant in Soho. After talking for a while, we found out that we had a lot in common – in fact, we seemed to have the same interests and tastes in everything. She smiled at me when I spoke to her, and when our eyes met this time I knew that I was head over heels in love with her. I thought that she was falling in love with me, too. We started going out with each other, and after some time we got engaged and decided to live together. We were both very happy and made plans to settle down and get married the following year.

However, it wasn't long before things started to go wrong. She seemed less affectionate and loving as the weeks passed, and I started to feel she was going off me. She criticized me all the time. 'Why are you always going on at me?' I asked.

In the end I wondered if we were suited to one another. I was keen on hard rock and she was fond of classical music. I was interested in sport and she was interested in politics. We finally fell out over a TV programme. We had a terrible row, broke off our engagement, and called off the wedding. A week later she moved out. I was heartbroken, and it took me a long time to get over it.

A few months later I heard she was engaged to a man who worked in local government. They got married, but after two years their marriage broke up and they got divorced.

I tell you this because last night I went to a party and I was drowning my sorrows when I saw her standing on the other side of the room sipping a glass of wine. I saw a man walk over to her and I heard him say, 'You seem to be on your own. Can I join you?'

Checking understanding

Match the verbs in A with the definitions in B.

A	B
1 to come across as something	a. to stop liking someone (informal)
2 to ask someone out somewhere	b. to start to live a stable, regular life in one place (perhaps after buying a house or getting married)
3 to go out with someone	c. to give the impression of having a particular characteristic
4 to settle down	d. to cancel something (an arrangement or event)
5 to go off someone	e. to discontinue something, to bring something to an abrupt end
6 to go on at someone	f. to spend time with someone socially, often to have a romantic relationship
7 to fall out (with someone) (over something)	g. to come to an end
8 to break something off	h. to have an argument with someone and stop being friendly with them
9 to call something off	i. to keep complaining about something to someone (informal)
10 to break up	j. to invite someone to go out somewhere (to a restaurant or theatre)

Drills

T.12a

Listen and respond to the prompts.

Practice

1   Jane is very upset. Her friend, Mary, has come to visit her. Look at their conversation below. Replace the words in *italics* with multi-word verbs.

Mary   What's the matter, Jane? Have you *had an argument with* Paul again?

Jane   Yes, you could say that . . .

Mary   Well, it takes two to have an argument. What was it about this time?

Jane   He said I was always *complaining and criticizing* him.

Mary   Is it true?

Jane   Well, in a way, yes. But I was feeling insecure because I thought he was *starting to dislike* me.

Mary   How long have you been *seeing* one another?

Jane   Nearly a year now. But yesterday I *discovered* he's been *having a relationship with* someone else.

Mary   Oh, so what did you do?

Jane   I told him, and he said he wanted to *end* our relationship.

Mary   But I thought you were planning to get married in June?

Jane   We've *cancelled* it.

Mary   Well, I'm sorry to hear the two of you have *ended your relationship*.

Jane   I think it'll take me a long time to *recover from* this.

Mary   Well, perhaps it's for the best. You were never really happy with him. And after all, there are plenty more fish in the sea!

T.12b

Listen to the dialogue to check your answers.

What does the last sentence of the dialogue mean? Why does Mary say it? How would you express the same idea in your own language?

Particles

2   There are six mistakes in the text below. Find them and correct them.

> I used to be very keen at football, but I lost interest in it when I met my best friend's sister. At first I was only fond on her, but later on I fell in love to her. We had a lot on common and thought about getting married. I was engaged with her for six months, but in the end she got married with someone else.

3 Work with your partner. Take turns asking one another the questions below. Try to use multi-word verbs in your questions and answers.

a. What impression do you think you give of yourself when you first meet people?
b. Imagine someone is always criticizing you. What would you do or say?
c. Would you have a relationship with someone your parents didn't approve of?
d. If you have a relationship with someone, how important is it that you both have a lot in common (that you are both keen on sport, for example)?
e. What kind of things make you stop liking someone?
f. What would make you end a relationship with someone?
g. When do you think is the right time to live a more quiet, stable life and get married?
h. Do you agree with the saying 'It's love which makes the world go round'? Why?/Why not?
i. Some people say 'True love never dies'. Do you agree? Why?/Why not?

Idiomatic expressions

4 Find the expressions in the text which mean the following:

1 to fall in love with someone the first time you see them
2 to be completely or deeply in love
3 to try to forget your troubles and disappointment by drinking alcohol

5 What do you think the following expressions mean?

1 the eternal triangle
2 an old flame
3 a one-sided relationship
4 There's no love lost between them.
5 a love–hate relationship

How multi-word verbs work
off
The particle *off* can be used with some verbs to give the idea of stopping or cancelling something:

*They **broke off** their engagement and **called off** the wedding.*

6 Complete the following sentences with multi-word verbs that use the particle *off*.

a. Can you _____ all the lights when you go to bed, please?
b. Hello, operator, I was talking to someone and we were _____ . Can you try to re-connect us, please?
c. There isn't time to have the meeting today, so we will have to _____ till next week.
d. It's been lovely talking to you on the phone, but I must _____ because there's someone at the front door. I'll call you again next week. Bye.
e. I wish they would make up their minds one way or the other. Yesterday they said the wedding was on, but now they've had another argument and say the wedding _____ .

What's the answer?

What is the difference between the following:

1 *to break something off* and *to break up?*
2 *to put something off* and *to call something off?*
3 *to call something off* and *to break something off?*

Jokes

He met her in a revolving door and has been going round with her ever since.

Mother A postcard came for you this morning, but there's no message on it.
Son Oh, yes, it's from my new girlfriend. She must be on holiday.
Mother How do you know it's from her? It's completely blank.
Son Because we're not on speaking terms at the moment.

Writing

Look at how the time expressions below are used to sequence the events in the story 'Across a crowded room'.

| At first | after a while | after some time | the following year |
| However, it wasn't long before | as the weeks passed | in the end |

Using these time expressions, as well as the multi-word verbs, idiomatic expressions, and prepositions you have learnt in this unit, write a description of *either*:

– a romantic play, book, or film that you know,
  or
– the development of a romantic relationship.

Tapescript section

Unit 1

Tapescript 1

Listen to the sentences. Then say the sentences again, using the multi-word verb prompts. The first one has been done for you.

1 Can I give you my homework tomorrow?
(hand in)
Can I hand in my homework tomorrow?
2 Can you check my homework to see if there are any mistakes?
(go through)
Can you go through my homework to see if there are any mistakes?
3 Could we postpone our meeting until tomorrow?
(put off)
Could we put off our meeting until tomorrow?
4 I must begin work.
(get down to)
I must get down to work.
5 I didn't pass the exam.
(get through)
I didn't get through the exam.
6 I passed my history exam with only 54%.
(scrape through)
I scraped through my history exam with only 54%.
7 Can I write down your name and address?
(take down)
Can I take down your name and address?
8 She's remaining at the same level as the other students in class.
(keep up with)
She's keeping up with the other students in class.
9 Everyone in class is making progress with their studies, but I'm getting worse and worse.
(fall behind)
Everyone in class is making progress with their studies, but I'm falling behind.
10 I must try to reach the same level as the other students in my class.
(catch up with)
I must try to catch up with the other students in my class.

Unit 2

Tapescript 2a

EA: Estate agent   **A:** Ann

EA Well, this is the flat. It's vacant at the moment. I'm afraid the previous owners didn't *look after* it very well, so it's not in perfect condition.
A Mmm . . .
EA As you can see, it's in need of some decoration and repair. There are four rooms altogether: kitchen, living room, bedroom, and bathroom. This is the living room. It hasn't been decorated recently.
A Yes, it certainly needs *doing up* . . . All the wallpaper is *coming off* the walls, and it's very cold and damp. How is the flat heated?
EA Well, there's an open fireplace, but it could be *taken out* and central heating could be *put in*.
A Mmm . . . It's not very large. I suppose I could *put up* some shelves for books and things. Do the carpets come with the flat?
EA Yes, though as you can see, they are rather old and don't add much value to the property.
A Yes, I agree. I think they all need *throwing out*, to be honest. What's that up there? Is that a hole in the ceiling?
EA Oh, yes, I'm afraid it is. I didn't notice that the last time I was here.
A Well, that will definitely need *seeing to* before it does any damage to the property.
EA Yes, of course. But I do think the flat has potential. It could look very good if it's *done up* nicely.
A Well, I'm certainly interested. Obviously I'll need to *talk it over* with my husband. You say it's vacant. Does that mean we could *move in* immediately?
EA Yes, the flat's empty so you could *move in* when you're ready.
A Well, I'll certainly *think it over* and if we decide to make an offer I'll call you tomorrow. Thank you for showing me round the flat.
EA No trouble, Mrs Jones. We hope to hear from you tomorrow then. Goodbye.
A Goodbye.

Tapescript 2b

Listen to the sentences. Then agree with them, using the multi-word verb prompts. The first one has been done for you.

1 This room looks terrible. It really needs decorating.
   (*do up*)
   Yes, it needs doing up.

2 Look, the wallpaper isn't sticking to the walls.
   (*come off*)
   Yes, it's coming off the walls.

3 That fireplace is very ugly. We could remove it.
   (*take out*)
   Yes, we could take it out.

4 The flat doesn't have any central heating. We must install it.
   (*put in*)
   Yes, we must put it in.

5 There are no shelves or cupboards. We could fix some to the walls.
   (*put up*)
   Yes, we could put some up.

6 There's a lot of rubbish in this room. It needs putting in the dustbin.
   (*throw out*)
   Yes, it needs throwing out.

7 The cooker doesn't work. It needs repairing.
   (*see to*)
   Yes, it needs seeing to.

8 We must discuss this before we decide.
   (*talk over*)
   Yes, we must talk it over.

9 We could start living here immediately.
   (*move in*)
   Yes, we could move in immediately.

10 We must consider it carefully before we decide.
   (*think over*)
   Yes, we must think it over.

Tapescript 2c

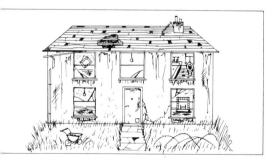

Here's a description of the house before it was done up.

Well, the roof's in a bad condition and needs repairing. There's an old fireplace but there's no central heating. The carpets downstairs have holes in them and there are no shelves or curtains.
The bathroom needs decorating and the bath itself is old-fashioned and rather ugly.
The old windows need replacing.
The outside walls of the house are cracked, so they need some attention.
The garden is in a terrible condition and it doesn't have a fence.
A new television aerial's needed.
And at the moment nobody's living there.

Tapescript 2d

a. I'd like to talk it over.
b. Did you throw them out?
c. They've decided to put it off.
d. We're going to do it up.
e. I'd like more time to think it over.
f. I didn't take it down.
g. Did you hand it in?
h. Can you help me put it up?

Unit 3

Tapescript 3a

Doc: Doctor
RB: Mr Rich Brown   **T:** Ms Teresa Green
LW: Mrs Lily White   **IR:** Mr Ivor Rose

1

Doc Hello, Mr Brown. And how are you?
RB Well, I haven't been feeling very well recently. I get out of breath very easily when I climb stairs or walk short distances, and last week I started getting pains in my chest.
Doc Mm, I see. Do you smoke?
RB Yes, I *get through* about 30 cigarettes a day.
Doc That's rather a lot. Have you tried giving up?
RB I have, doctor, but I can't break the habit.
Doc Well, I think you should at least try to *cut down on* the amount you smoke. What about your eating habits? Have you *put on* any weight recently?
RB Yes, I'm a little overweight at the moment. You see, I eat in cafés most of the time and I tend to drive everywhere because of my job. I sell sports equipment.
Doc Well, it sounds as if you're out of condition. I think you need to take some regular exercise.

RB What, you mean *take up* jogging?

Doc Well, jogging or something like that, but the most important thing is, I think you need to lose some weight, so I want you to go on a diet.

RB Go on a diet?

Doc Yes, it's particularly important that you *cut out* fatty foods. What about alcohol? How much do you drink?

RB About two or three pints of beer in the evenings.

Doc I think you need to *cut out* drinking completely for the next few months.

RB That's easier said than done, doctor.

Doc I agree, but if you don't change your lifestyle, you could be in trouble . . .

2

Doc Hello, Teresa. And what seems to be the problem?

T Well, I'm not feeling very well at the moment. I'm preparing for exams and I've been staying up late at night studying. This morning I got out of bed very early to do some more work, and I *passed out*. My flatmate found me on the floor. I *came round* after a few seconds.

Doc Mm. Have you had any other symptoms?

T Well, I have been feeling a bit off colour and sometimes I get splitting headaches. What do you think is wrong with me?

Doc Well, it sounds as if you've been burning the candle at both ends. You've probably been overdoing it and you're overtired. I don't think it's anything to worry about, but I think you should take it easy for a while and try to get enough sleep.

T Yes, I haven't been getting much sleep lately.

Doc I'll give you something to help you relax in the evenings. And just try to have a few early nights.

T Thank you, doctor.

3

Doc Hello, it's Mrs White, isn't it?

LW That's right, doctor.

Doc What can I do for you?

LW Oh dear. I'm always tired, doctor – I'm absolutely worn out at the end of the day.

Doc Are you eating regular meals?

LW Well, I don't really have time to eat – I'm too busy with the children. And we don't have much money for food because my husband's out of work.

Doc It sounds to me as if you're a bit run down. I'll write out a prescription for some extra iron and vitamins, and I'd like you to come back in a couple of weeks so I can see how you're getting on.

LW Thank you, doctor.

4

Doc Hello, Mr Rose. How are you feeling?

IR I feel a bit under the weather. I've got a headache and I ache all over.

Doc Mm. You've probably *picked something up*. Let me see. Yes, you're running a temperature. I think you're *going down with* flu.

IR How long will it take me to *get over* it? You see, I need to get back to work as soon as possible.

Doc About four or five days. I'll write out a prescription for some pain killers for you. Take these tablets three times a day after meals. Meanwhile, my advice is to go to bed with a hot water bottle and drink lots of fluids. After a few days you should feel as right as rain.

Tapescript 3b

1 How long will it take me to *get over* it?

2 I think you're *going down with* flu.

3 I *get through* about 30 cigarettes a day.

4 You've probably *picked something up*.

5 It's particularly important that you *cut out* fatty foods.

6 Have you *put on* any weight recently?

7 What, you mean *take up* jogging?

8 I think you should try to *cut down on* the amount you smoke.

9 I *passed out*. My flatmate found me on the floor.

10 I *came round* after a few seconds.

Tapescript 3c

Listen to the sentences. Then say the sentences again, using the multi-word verb prompts. The first one has been done for you.

1 Achoo! Oh dear, I think I'm starting to catch a cold.
   (*come down with*)
   Achoo! Oh dear, I think I'm coming down with a cold.

2 I think I caught my cold from Jim.
   (*pick up*)
   I think I picked up my cold from Jim.

3 It took me a week to recover from my last cold.
   (*get over*)
   It took me a week to get over my last cold.

4 I really must reduce the amount I smoke.
   (*cut down on*)
   I really must cut down on the amount I smoke.

5 I smoke 20 cigarettes a day.
   (*get through*)
   I get through 20 cigarettes a day.

6 My weight has increased recently.
   (*put on*)
   I've put on weight recently.

7 I must stop eating chips.
   (*cut out*)
   I must cut out eating chips.
8 I've started playing golf as a hobby.
   (*take up*)
   I've taken up golf as a hobby.
9 I think I'm going to faint.
   (*pass out*)
   I think I'm going to pass out.
10 I recovered consciousness a few seconds later.
   (*come round*)
   I came round a few seconds later.

Unit 4

Tapescript 4

Listen to the sentences. Then say the sentences again, using the multi-word verb prompts. The first one has been done for you.

1 I can't tolerate that noise any longer!
   (*put up with*)
   I can't put up with that noise any longer!
2 You can visit us any time.
   (*drop in on*)
   You can drop in on us any time.
3 We leave our flat on Friday.
   (*move out*)
   We move out on Friday.
4 Can I quickly read your history notes?
   (*look through*)
   Can I look through your history notes?
5 The curtains don't match the wallpaper.
   (*go with*)
   The curtains don't go with the wallpaper.
6 Could you let me sleep in your house on Saturday night?
   (*put up*)
   Could you put me up on Saturday night?
7 I found by accident an old love letter you sent me two years ago.
   (*come across*)
   I came across an old love letter you sent me two years ago.
8 These flowers will help to make the room look brighter.
   (*brighten up*)
   These flowers will help to brighten up the room.
9 From my bedroom window I can see a garden full of flowers.
   (*look out onto*)
   My bedroom window looks out onto a garden full of flowers.

Unit 5

Tapescript 5a

1

I: Interviewer   J: Jean

I Hello. I work for Sun Tour holidays and I'm interviewing people about their last holiday. Would you mind answering a few questions for our survey?
J No, not at all.
I Thank you. Firstly, could you tell me about your travel arrangements? Did you experience any difficulties in reaching your destination?
J Well, our plane didn't *take off* on time. It was delayed five hours, so we didn't get to Cyprus until three in the morning and we were very tired when we got there. But there was a coach at the airport waiting to *pick us up* and it *dropped us off* at the hotel in time for breakfast, so that was all right.
I And how was the hotel?
J Well, we were a little disappointed with the room. It didn't have a balcony and it *looked out onto* some rather ugly, noisy streets, but the beach was *just a stone's throw away* – it only took us a couple of minutes to get there.
I And how important are holidays to you?
J Oh, we always look forward to going on holiday. We always make sure we *get away* at least once a year.

2

I: Interviewer   A: Andy

I Could you tell me first about your travel arrangements? Did you have any problems with them?
A We had no problems flying out, but coming back was awful. We *checked out* of the hotel early Saturday morning and *set off* for the airport by taxi. We were supposed to *get back* to London in the afternoon, but our plane didn't *touch down* until Sunday at four in the morning, so we were absolutely worn out when we got home.
I Oh, and why was there such a delay?
A Technical difficulties, they said. Something wrong with the engine.
I And apart from that, how was the rest of the holiday?
A Oh, it was great. I took up windsurfing and I want to go back and do it again next year.
I And how important are holidays to you?
A I think they're important. You need a change, you need to see somewhere different. *Travel broadens the mind*, doesn't it?

3

I: Interviewer   S: Susan

I And what was your last holiday like?

S Marvellous, absolutely marvellous. We went to Rome and we met up with some very nice people from Manchester. We *looked round* the city together and saw all the sights – the Colosseum and St. Peter's . . . And on the way back to England we *stopped off* in Paris and spent a couple of days there. We had a marvellous time.

I And how important are holidays to you?

S Oh, it's good to *get away from it all* and forget all your worries and problems, even if it's only for a few days.

4

I: Interviewer   S: Sheila

I So could you tell me about your last holiday?

S It was a complete disaster, and it was a pity, because I was really looking forward *to* it. The plane didn't *take off* on time – it was delayed six hours! The flight was awful – I suffered *from* air-sickness all the way. My hotel room was small and dirty. I complained *about* it *to* the manager and I insisted *on* having a different room, and I even succeeded *in* getting one, but it was just the same!

I Goodness, it sounds terrible.

S I was really disappointed *with* the beach – it was ugly and miles from the hotel. No, the whole thing was a complete disaster. In the end I couldn't wait to *get back* home.

I So you weren't at all satisfied *with* your holiday?

S No, I wasn't. I'd never go back there again!

I And how important are holidays to you?

S Very. I love visiting beautiful places. That's why I was so angry *about* the holiday and *with* the man who booked it for me.

I Yes, I'm sure you were. Which company did you book your holiday with?

S Sun Tour Holidays.

I Oh . . .

Tapescript 5b

1 Our plane didn't *take off* on time. It was delayed five hours.

2 But there was a coach at the airport waiting to *pick us up* and it *dropped us off* at the hotel in time for breakfast.

3 We always make sure we *get away* at least once a year.

4 We *checked out* of the hotel early Saturday morning and *set off* for the airport by taxi.

5 We were supposed to *get back* to London in the afternoon.

6 Our plane didn't *touch down* until Sunday at four in the morning.

7 We *looked round* the city together and saw all the sights – the Colosseum and St. Peter's.

8 On the way back to England we *stopped off* in Paris and spent a couple of days there.

Tapescript 5c

Listen to the sentences. Decide what you would say in each situation, using multi-word verbs from this unit. The first sentence has been done for you.

1 You are at the airport and you want to know what time the plane departs. What do you say?
   What time does the plane take off?

2 You are going on a coach trip with some friends and you want to know what time it starts. What do you say?
   What time do we set off?

3 Your friend is giving you a lift in her car. You want her to let you out at the station. What do you say?
   Can you drop me off at the station?

4 Your friend is going out and you want to know what time she will return. What do you say?
   What time will you get back?

5 You want your friend to collect you by car at 6.00 o'clock. What do you say?
   Can you pick me up at 6.00 o'clock?

6 You are staying at a hotel and you want to know what time you have to vacate your room. You go to the receptionist. What do you say?
   What time do I have to check out?

7 You are on a plane flying to Madrid and you want to know what time the plane lands. What do you say?
   What time does the plane touch down in Madrid?

8 You are going to Oxford to see a play and you want to know if there will be time to see the town. What do you say?
   Will there be time to look round the town?

9 You are on your way home with a friend. You want to suggest that you both go into a bar for a drink. What do you say?
   Shall we stop off for a/and have a drink?

10 Last summer you did extra work for your boss instead of going on holiday. He asks you if you would like to do the same thing this year. You think you need to have a holiday this summer. What do you say?
   I think I need to get away this summer.

Unit 6

Tapescript 6b

Listen to the sentences. Then say the sentences again, using the multi-word verb prompts. The first one has been done for you.

1 I have always admired and respected my father.
   (*look up to*)
   I have always looked up to my father.

2 The little boy said he wanted to be a train driver when he was older.
   (*grow up*)
   The little boy said he wanted to be a train driver when he grew up.

3 She's very similar to her mother – they are both very intelligent.
   (*take after*)
   She takes after her mother. They are both very intelligent.

4 I often think about my childhood.
   (*look back on*)
   I often look back on my childhood.

5 I can't make her listen to me or understand what I'm trying to say.
   (*get through to*)
   I can't get through to her.

6 When her mother died, she was raised by her aunt.
   (*bring up*)
   When her mother died, she was brought up by her aunt.

7 How can we avoid going to my brother's party?
   (*get out of*)
   How can we get out of going to my brother's party?

8 He was not punished for using bad language at home.
   (*get away with*)
   He got away with using bad language at home.

9 At first her father wouldn't let her go to the all-night party, but in the end she persuaded him to let her go.
   (*get round*)
   She got round her father.

10 She reprimanded him for breaking the window.
   (*tell off*)
   She told him off for breaking the window.

Tapescript 6c

Listen to the problems. Try to answer the questions, using a multi-word verb from this unit.

1 You want your boss to give you a day off work. What would you do?
   Try to get round him or her.

2 Your boss wants you to do some extra work, but you are very busy. What would you do?
   Try to get out of doing it.

Unit 7

Tapescript 7a

The Emperor's new clothes

Many years ago there was an Emperor who spent all his time and money on *dressing up* in expensive clothes. He loved riding round in his wonderful garments so that everybody could see him. He didn't care about his country very much because he was much more interested in what was in or out of fashion. His palace was full of wardrobes containing clothes he had worn only once.

One day two dishonest men appeared at the palace and said they could make beautiful clothes which had magical properties. Only clever people would be able to see them – they would be invisible to anyone who was stupid or not good at their job. The Emperor thought this was an excellent opportunity to find out who was wise and who was foolish in his kingdom, and whether or not people were suitable for their jobs. He gave the two men a large sum of money and told them to start work immediately.

The two men were given gold and silver thread (which they put in their pockets and kept for themselves) and they started making the clothes. They pretended to work hard all day and night, though of course there was nothing on their weaving machines – they were empty! Soon everyone in the city knew about their work and the magical properties of the clothes they were making, and they all wanted to find out if their neighbours were stupid or not.

After several weeks the Emperor wanted to know how they were getting on. How much progress had they made? When would the clothes be ready? He decided to send an old and honest minister, who was certainly clever and good at his job, to visit the two men.

The minister entered the room where the two men were working. They looked very busy – they were cutting and sewing with great energy – but to his horror, he couldn't see what they were working on! It was as if they were cutting the air with large scissors and sewing it together!

'Ah, we're so pleased you've come', said one of the men. 'The work is going well, as you can see, and it should be finished by the end of the week.' And the man showed him the different colours and patterns of the materials as

81

if they were in front of his eyes. The minister blinked and could still see nothing. 'Goodness!' he thought to himself, 'I must be stupid! I can't see a thing! I must be careful not to let anyone find out or they will think I'm stupid and I will lose my job.'

'Oh, marvellous!' he said. 'What beautiful colours! What wonderful patterns! I've never seen anything like it!' He returned to the Emperor and told him the clothes were the most beautiful he'd ever seen. The Emperor sent a second minister and the same thing happened. So he made up his mind to go and see the clothes for himself, taking all his ministers with him.

On entering the room, the Emperor found the two men looking very proud of themselves. 'We've finished,' they said. 'Here you are. What do you think of them? Aren't they the most beautiful clothes you've ever seen?' The Emperor saw nothing. The men acted as if they were holding clothes, and all the ministers smiled and nodded and commented on the patterns and designs – but he saw nothing. 'I must be stupid!', thought the Emperor. 'Everyone else can see them – but I can't. Nobody must find out!'

'Yes, these are beautiful clothes indeed!' said the Emperor. 'What wonderful colours and designs!'
'Would you like to *try them on?*' said one of the men. 'We need to see if they fit. We must check they are not too big or too small.'
So the Emperor *took off* his clothes and *put on* the invisible clothes. He had no difficulty in *getting into* them. He stood in front of the mirror and said 'Yes, they fit perfectly.' And all the ministers around him agreed.

'Look, your majesty,' said one of the men, 'You have forgotten to *do up* one of the buttons.'
'Oh, yes,' said the Emperor with an embarrassed laugh. 'I didn't see it.' And he pretended to *do up* the button.
'These clothes will last forever,' said one of the men. 'They'll never *wear out.*'

Then one of the ministers suggested there should be a procession through the city so that everyone could see the Emperor's new clothes and admire them. There was no way out for the Emperor because he knew he could not refuse. He would have to *go through* with it.

The next day the procession took place and everyone shouted and cheered. 'What wonderful clothes!' they all said to one another. 'How well the colours go with the Emperor's crown!' But one small boy said 'Look! The Emperor *has nothing on*! – he isn't wearing any clothes!' The people around the boy heard this and started

whispering, and soon everybody was saying 'He*'s got nothing on*!' The Emperor heard them, but he thought 'I must not stop. I must *carry on* or it will ruin the procession.' So he continued walking along even more proudly than before, with his ministers helping to carry his invisible clothes.

(Adapted from Hans Andersen's fairy tale)

Tapescript 7b

Listen to the sentences. Decide what you would say in the following situations.

1 It's very cold outside and your friend is about to leave without a coat. What do you say?
   You'd better put a coat on.
2 You have been invited to an important dinner party. You are not sure if you need to wear very smart clothes or not. What do you say?
   Do I need to dress up for the occasion?
3 A man comes to your house to repair the TV. His shoes are very dirty. You want him to remove them before he comes in. What do you say?
   Could you take your shoes off, please?
4 You are in a clothes shop and you see a nice pair of trousers. You are not sure if they are the right size or if they'll suit you. What do you say to the shop assistant?
   Can I try these trousers on, please?
5 You can't fasten the button on your shirt. You ask for help. What do you say?
   Can you do this button up for me, please?
6 You look at your shoes and you see there are holes in them. What do you say?
   My shoes are worn out/My shoes are wearing out.
7 You have been asked to make a speech in front of a large audience. At the last moment you feel very nervous and decide you can't do it. What do you say?
   I can't go through with it.
8 You're trying to put on some shoes but they are too small for you. What do you say?
   I can't get into these shoes.
9 You are asked if you want to continue studying at college or leave and find a job. You want to continue your studies. What do you say?
   I want to carry on with my studies.
10 You saw a thief in a green jumper and blue jeans. The police ask you what he was wearing. What do you say?
   He had on a green jumper and blue jeans.

apescript 7c

W1: Woman 1   W2: Woman 2

W1 Well, what do you think of this one?

W2 Mm. It doesn't really *go with* the colour of your jumper. Why don't you *try on* the red skirt?

W1 OK . . . Goodness, I can't *get into* it. And if I do, I won't be able to *do the buttons up*. It's no good. I'll have to go on a diet.

W2 What about this one? I think this is fantastic! You'll look *out of this world* in it.

W1 Do you think so?

M: Man   A: Shop assistant

A Hello, can I help you?

M Yes, please, I'd like to *try on* these trousers.

A Of course, sir. The changing rooms are just over there.

H: Husband   W: Wife

W Aren't you going to get changed?

H No, I'm going like this.

W You can't go looking like that.

H Well I'm not going to *dress up* just to have dinner with my parents.

W That's not the point. That shirt's filthy, and it's *worn out*. Look, it's got holes in it. *Take it off* and *put on* that one I gave you for Christmas.

W: Woman   A: Shop assistant

W Excuse me, I can't *get my foot into* this shoe. Can I *try on* a size 6?

A I'm afraid you're *out of luck*, madam. We're completely *out of stock* in that particular size.

Unit 8

apescript 8

Listen to the sentences. Then say the sentences again, using the multi-word verb prompts. The first one has been done for you.

1 Can you extinguish that cigarette, please?
   (*put out*)
   Can you put out that cigarette, please?

2 The alarm bell started ringing.
   (*go off*)
   The alarm bell went off.

3 I shouted his name loudly but he didn't hear me.
   (*call out*)
   I called out his name but he didn't hear me.

4 The police are investigating the accident.
   (*look into*)
   The police are looking into the accident.

5 Come quickly – a fire has started!
   (*break out*)
   Come quickly – a fire has broken out!

6 He experienced a lot of pain.
   (*go through*)
   He went through a lot of pain.

7 He started the fire alarm by accident.
   (*set off*)
   He set off the fire alarm by accident.

8 The government has said that tax cuts are not possible.
   (*rule out*)
   The government has ruled out tax cuts.

9 The prisoners escaped through the window.
   (*get out*)
   The prisoners got out through the window.

10 I think we should ask for the help of a doctor.
   (*call in*)
   I think we should call in a doctor.

Unit 9

Tapescript 9a

Jeremy

At the moment I have a very good, well-paid job that I enjoy doing, but it hasn't always been like this.

Several years ago I used to work as a salesman for a small company that specialized in making motor components for the car industry. It was the sort of job where you had to be committed to your product, you had to believe in it and do everything possible to sell it. But times were hard, and a lot of companies were going out of business, so our company started to *cut back* on the number of people it employed in order to save money – fortunately, I wasn't one of them – but in the end it had to *close down*, and I found myself out of work for the first time in my life. I applied for several jobs in similar companies, but I wasn't successful – every one of them *turned me down*.

Then one day I was looking through the paper and I came across an advertisement for courses that specialized in journalism. I filled in an application form, sent it off, was accepted onto the course, studied hard, passed my exams, and became a qualified journalist. I then wrote to a small magazine for the car industry, attended an interview along with dozens of other applicants and, to my surprise, they *took me on*. The magazine grew in size and popularity, I moved from writing articles to being sub-editor, and this year I became the editor, so I suppose I've been lucky really.

Angela

When I was young my father always told me how important it was to *get on* in life and be a success. 'You must make something of your life,' he used to say. I think he wanted me to be a doctor or an engineer or something like that. And I can remember how disappointed he was when I left school early and started work as a secretary.

It was a small, badly-run company, and when I went there they told me the job wasn't difficult and I would soon *pick it up*. At the beginning I liked the job, but as time passed the work started to *take up* more of my time and I found I was working late in the evenings and even at weekends. And in addition to this I had to put up with poor working conditions and a low salary – I earned just enough to *get by* – and there were no promotion prospects at all. All this really *got me down*. And then I started to wonder if I was really cut out for this kind of work – it didn't really suit me or my particular abilities.

Then one day – I remember I'd been working very hard that month and had put in a lot of extra hours – I went to see my boss to ask for some time off work. I needed to visit my mother, who wasn't well at the time. I have to say that I didn't get on with my boss very well. Anyway, he refused point-blank. He said it was out of the question and he didn't want to hear another word. I tried explaining but I just couldn't get through to him. He wouldn't listen. So I walked out of the office, and as far as I was concerned, that was it, that was the last straw. The next day I handed in my resignation, and I said to myself I would never put myself in that kind of position again. I decided to return to studying and *go in for* law. I graduated from London University and now I'm starting to make my way in the world. As my father used to say, 'The world is my oyster'.

So was my father right? Is it important to *get on* in the world? Well, in some ways it is, but it depends on how you measure success and what you want to get out of life. After all, there are other things in life besides work.

Tapescript 9b

Listen to the sentences. Then say the sentences again, using the multi-word verb prompts. The first one has been done for you.

1 The company has employed extra staff.
(*take on*)
The company has taken on extra staff.
2 I've decided to make a career in medicine.
(*go in for*)
I've decided to go in for medicine.
3 She survives on a very small income.
(*get by*)
She gets by on a very small income.
4 He didn't accept my offer of help.
(*turn down*)
He turned down my offer of help.
5 The factory will have to reduce production.
(*cut back on*)
The factory will have to cut back on production.
6 The bad working conditions depress me.
(*get me down*)
The bad working conditions get me down.
7 The company has stopped doing business.
(*close down*)
The company has closed down.
8 I learnt some Arabic while I was in Cairo.
(*pick up*)
I picked up some Arabic while I was in Cairo.
9 She wants to be a success in her job.
(*get on*)
She wants to get on in her job.
10 Writing reports uses a lot of my time.
(*take up*)
Writing reports takes up a lot of my time.

Tapescript 9c

1

I'm often on duty at weekends, especially if there is a football match or a demonstration. I'm there to see things don't get out of control. I think you have to be cut out for this type of work because it isn't easy and can be dangerous. You serve the public and you're there to protect them, but they don't always appreciate what you're trying to do. The pay and conditions are all right, which is a good thing because you can't go on strike.

2

Sometimes I'm on duty all night and it isn't easy to take time off work. The salary isn't very good – I can get by o it – but I'd never go on strike, because it's my job to look

ter people and I know they depend on me. Sometimes
ou have to put up with bad working conditions but you
now that what you're doing is an extremely worthwhile
b.

ell, basically I pick people up and I drop them off. I take
em where they want to go to and that's it.

ou have to be cut out for this kind of work, otherwise
ou shouldn't go in for it. You have to learn a lot of
ings by heart, and you can suffer from nerves
roughout the whole of your professional life. You are
ten out of work and you have to be very ambitious and
cky to get on, but if you do, the world's your oyster.

ou have to be good at getting on with people, and you
ave to remain calm at all times – you must never panic.
ou need some training for this job, but some things you
an pick up quite quickly. It's exciting to stop off in exotic
laces and look round for a few days, but sometimes the
ork can be very routine and the pay is average.

ou have to work long hours, and you can be on call
venty-four hours a day, but it's wonderful to be able to
se your knowledge to help people and relieve suffering. I
ink people tend to look up to you as a result.

ke all professionals, you have to be committed to what
ou're doing. I'm at work very early in the morning to set
ings up so that everything is ready when the day starts.
he work takes up a lot of my time, especially preparation
me and going through people's work and correcting it.
he poor pay sometimes gets me down, but I believe in
hat I'm doing and that's the most important thing.

nit 10

apescript 10

sten to the sentences. Decide what you would say in
ach situation, using the multi-word verb prompts. The
rst one has been done for you.

1 You look in the fridge and see there is no milk. What
do you say?
(run out of)
We've run out of milk.

2 You arrive late for a meeting because you were
delayed in a traffic jam. What do you say?
(hold up)
I'm sorry I'm late. I was held up in a traffic jam.

3 You want to know if your parents will come with you
to the airport to say goodbye when you leave. What
do you say to them?
(see off)
Will you see me off at the airport?

4 Your friend is reading a letter but the handwriting is
not very clear. She asks you to try and read one of the
words for her. You try but you can't. What do you
say?
(make out)
I'm sorry, I can't make it out.

5 You are talking to someone at a motorway restaurant.
He tells you he is driving north. You want to know
what his destination is. What do you say?
(head for)
Where are you heading for?

6 You're in a taxi and you want the driver to stop
outside the bank. What do you say?
(pull up)
Can you pull up outside the bank, please?

7 You're in your car on the motorway and it stops
working. You phone a garage for help. What do you
say?
(break down)
*My car has broken down on the motorway. Can you help
me, please?*

8 You want the driver of another car to move his car
closer to the side of the road so that you can pass in
your car. What do you say?
(pull over)
Can you pull over, please?

9 You are in your friend's car and you see another car
begin to move out in front of you. You want to warn
your friend. What do you say?
(pull out)
Watch out! That car's going to pull out!

10 You are in your friend's car and your friend isn't
driving very carefully. You are frightened the journey
will end with you both in hospital. What do you say?
(end up)
If you don't drive more carefully, we'll end up in hospital.

Unit 11

Tapescript 11a

Here is the seven o'clock news. First, the news headlines.

- Thieves *break in* at the Royal Gallery
- Ship goes down at sea near the Sussex coast
- Three men *break out* of Brixton prison
- Plane comes down in jungle
- Chemical factory *blows up*
- Severe weather cuts off towns in the north
- Damaged plane touches down safely

Now here is the news in detail.

Thieves break in at the Royal Gallery

Last night thieves *broke into* the Royal Gallery and *got away with* paintings worth over a quarter of a million pounds. The break-in happened around 11.00 o'clock in the evening, but was not discovered until the early hours of the morning. At present it is not known how the thieves got into the building, though a security guard is helping the police with their enquiries.

Ship goes down at sea near the Sussex coast

A ship has gone down at sea off the south coast of England following an explosion in its engine room. The ship was carrying a cargo of wood and was heading for Liverpool. The fire spread rapidly and was soon out of control. However, all the crew were *picked up* safely by the rescue services.

Three men break out of Brixton prison

Three men *broke out of* Brixton prison this morning. They overpowered a prison officer and escaped by climbing over the wall. They were seen *making off* in a red car that was waiting for them outside the prison. One of the men was later picked up by the police, but the other two men are still on the run. Police have warned the public not to approach these men, as they may be armed and dangerous.

Plane comes down in jungle

A plane with two English passengers on board has come down in dense jungle in Brazil. It seems that one of the engines *cut out* while the plane was heading for Rio de Janeiro, and the pilot was forced to make a crash landing in the jungle. A rescue team is now searching for survivors.

Chemical factory blows up

News is coming in of an explosion at a chemical processing plant in Luton. It seems that part of the factory *blew up* and a fire has broken out. Although the fire is dying down and the situation is under control, the fire brigade say they won't be able to put it out completely for several hours.

Severe weather cuts off towns in the north

Severe weather conditons in the north of England have *cut off* several towns and villages. Many roads are impassable due to heavy falls of snow. Supplies of food are being flown into some villages by helicopter.

Damaged plane touches down safely

A plane had to make an emergency landing at Heathrow this morning when one of its doors blew off. Shortly after taking off an explosion was heard and the plane had to turn back to Heathrow. The emergency services were *standing by* in case of a crash landing, but the plane touched down safely.

'I never want to go through an experience like that again!' said the passenger who had been sitting next to the door. 'I don't think I'll ever get over the shock of seeing the door come off and a drop of 1,000 metres beneath me!'

Tapescript 11b

Listen to the sentences. Then say the sentences again, using the multi-word verb prompts. The first one has been done for you.

1 The engine keeps stopping.
   (*cut out*)
   The engine keeps cutting out.
2 The survivors were rescued from the sea by helicopter.
   (*pick up*)
   The survivors were picked up by helicopter.
3 Don't touch it! It might explode!
   (*blow up*)
   Don't touch it! It might blow up!
4 He was arrested by the police for possessing drugs.
   (*pick up*)
   He was picked up by the police for possessing drugs.
5 The police are ready for action in case there is trouble.
   (*stand by*)
   The police are standing by in case there is trouble.
6 Someone entered our house illegally at the weekend.
   (*break into*)
   Someone broke into our house at the weekend.

86

7 Our village was isolated by a snowstorm for a week.
(cut off)
Our village was cut off by a snowstorm for a week.

8 He's escaped from prison again.
(break out)
He's broken out of prison again.

9 The robbers succeeded in stealing over £100,000.
(get away with)
The robbers got away with over £100,000.

0 I tried to stop the thief, but he escaped on a motorbike.
(make off)
I tried to stop the thief, but he made off on a motorbike.

Unit 12

Tapescript 12a

Listen to the sentences. Then say the sentences again, using the multi-word verb prompts. The first one has been done for you.

1 The concert has been cancelled.
(call off)
The concert has been called off.

2 Stop criticizing me all the time!
(go on at)
Stop going on at me all the time!

3 He's invited her to the cinema.
(ask out)
He's asked her out to the cinema.

4 Julie is having a relationship with a man from France.
(go out with)
Julie is going out with a man from France.

5 He gives the impression of being rather aggressive.
(come across as)
He comes across as rather aggressive.

6 Their marriage has ended.
(break up)
Their marriage has broken up.

7 Michael has had an argument with Tony and isn't talking to him.
(fall out with)
Michael has fallen out with Tony.

8 I want to have a stable life, buy a house, and get married.
(settle down)
I want to settle down.

9 They have ended their relationship.
(break off)
They have broken off their relationship.

10 I'm starting to dislike him.
(go off)
I'm starting to go off him.

Tapescript 12b

M: Mary **J:** Jane

M What's the matter, Jane? Have you *fallen out with* Paul again?

J Yes, you could say that . . .

M Well, it takes two to have an argument. What was it about this time?

J He said I was always *going on at* him.

M Is it true?

J Well, in a way, yes. But I was feeling insecure because I thought he was *going off* me.

M How long have you been *going out with* one another?

J Nearly a year now. But yesterday I *found out* he's been *going out with* someone else.

M Oh, so what did you do?

J I told him, and he said he wanted to *break off* our relationship.

M But I thought you were planning to get married in June?

J We've *called it off.*

M Well, I'm sorry to hear the two of you have *broken up.*

J I think it'll take me a long time to *get over* this.

M Well, perhaps it's for the best. You were never really happy with him. And after all, there are plenty more fish in the sea!

Answer key

Introductory unit

1 *to look for someone/something* = to try to find someone/something

to look out = (to tell someone) to be careful (usually imperative)

to look down on someone = to consider someone inferior

2 a. L

b. N *to run out of something* = to have no more of something

c. L

d. L

e. N *to look into something* = to investigate something

f. L

g. N *to look through something* = to read something, usually quickly

h. N *to put something on* = to cause something electrical to begin working

i. L

j. N *to go over something* = to repeat something in order to teach or learn it

3 The particle *over* in all the example sentences suggests the idea of something falling or being pushed to the ground. The particle *down* can have almost the same meaning with all these verbs except for *trip over*.

4 1 d. 2 a. 3 c. 4 b.

6 a. Type 3
b. Type 1
c. Type 1
d. Type 2
e. Type 1
f. Type 3
g. Type 2
h. Type 3
i. Type 2
j. Type 1

7

Type 1	Type 2	Type 3	Type 4
run out	hold	fall over	get on
fall over	something	something	with
come	up		something
round	push		run out of
	someone/		something
	something		put up
	over		with
			someone/
			something
			get on
			with
			someone

Unit 1 Getting down to work

Checking understanding

1 1 b. 2 h. 3 i. 4 a. 5 g. 6 c. 7 d. 8 j. 9 f. 10 e.

2 1 Number 9 is falling behind/not keeping up with the others.

2 Number 6 is keeping up with number 2.

3 Number 5 is catching up with number 4.

Practice

2 to have difficulty in (do*ing*) something
to have problems *with* (do*ing*) something
to concentrate *on* (do*ing*) something
to be good/quite good
    not good/bad   at (do*ing*) something
    awful/hopeless

Idiomatic expressions

4 *to pass with flying colours* = to pass an exam with high marks

5 *a piece of cake* = something that is very easy to do (informal)

Two heads are better than one. = More ideas or solutions will be produced if you work with someone else rather than on your own.

to burn the midnight oil = to work or study late into the night

by the skin of my teeth = to just manage to do something (but nearly fail)

to learn something by heart = to learn something so that you can remember it perfectly, word for word. Another way of saying this is 'to commit something to memory'.

to learn something parrot fashion = to repeat words or ideas without understanding their meaning. It has a strongly negative connotation. We can also say 'to parrot something'.

How multi-word verbs work

7 a. a piece of cake
  b. Two heads are better than one.
  c. burn the midnight oil
  d. pass with flying colours

8 get through, scrape through
  1 go/look/read through
  2 note/write/put down
  3 think through
    get through

What's the answer?

To catch up with something or someone means that you are behind and making an effort to be at the same level, but *to keep up with* something or someone means you are already at the same level but making an effort to remain in that position.

Unit 2 Looking round a flat

Presentation

1 The whole flat needs doing up:
  – it needs decorating
  – new wallpaper needs to be put up
  – central heating could be put in
  – the old carpets need throwing out
  – the hole in the ceiling needs seeing to.
2 Ann doesn't decide to buy it. She wants time to think it over and then talk it over with her husband.

Checking understanding

1 a. doing up
  b. was coming off
  c. took it out
  d. put in
  e. put up
  f. threw them out
  g. seeing to
  h. talk it over
  i. move in
  j. think it over

Practice

1 – The roof has been seen to.
  – The old fireplace has been taken out and central heating has been put in.
  – The old carpets downstairs have been thrown out.
  – New shelves and curtains have been put up.
  – The bathroom has been done up and a new bath has been put in.
  – The old windows have been taken out and new ones have been put in.
  – The outside walls of the house have been seen to.
  – The garden has been seen to and a new fence has been put up.
  – A new television aerial has been put up.
  – Some people have moved in.

need + gerund

2 b. needs seeing to/needs to be seen to
  c. need putting up/need to be put up
  d. needs throwing out/needs to be thrown out
  e. needs doing up/needs to be done up
  f. needs putting in/needs to be put in

Idiomatic expressions

3 1 *Home, sweet home:* used to show pleasure when one is returning home after a period of absence.
  2 *An Englishman's home is his castle:* no one can enter an Englishman's home without permission and nobody can tell him how to behave there.
  3 *Make yourself at home:* an invitation to someone to make themselves comfortable and behave as if they were in their own home.
  4 *It's home from home:* a place as pleasant and comfortable as one's own home.

4 a. make yourself at home   c. Home, sweet home
  b. home from home   d. An Englishman's home is his castle.

How multi-word verbs work

5 a. I'd like to talk it over.
  b. Did you throw them out?
  c. They've decided to put it off.
  d. We're going to do it up.
  e. I'd like more time to think it over.
  f. I didn't take it down.
  g. Did you hand it in?
  h. Can you help me put them up?

6 Stress rule: With Type 2 multi-word verbs the particle is stressed when it is separated from the verb.

What's the answer?

to take something out = to remove something, but *to throw something out* = to dispose of it.

Speaking

2 *There's no place like home* = home is the best place, nowhere else is like it.

Unit 3 Healthy body, healthy mind

Preparation

Healthy body, healthy mind = physical health and mental health go together.

Presentation

Mr Brown Symptoms: he gets out of breath easily, pains in his chest
    Diagnosis: out of condition, eats badly, smokes and drinks too much
    Treatment: regular exercise – take up jogging, cut down on smoking, cut out fatty foods and drink
Ms Green Symptoms: she passed out, she came round after a few seconds, feeling off colour and splitting headaches
    Diagnosis: she's been burning the candle at both ends, not getting enough sleep
    Treatment: take it easy for a while, something to help her relax in the evenings
Mrs White Symptoms: she's always tired and worn out
    Diagnosis: she's run down
    Treatment: extra iron and vitamins
Mr Rose Symptoms: feels under the weather, headache, aches all over, running a temperature
    Diagnosis: picked up something, going down with flu
    Treatment: tablets three times a day, go to bed with a hot water bottle, drink fluids

Checking understanding

1 b. 2 c. 3 d. 4 i. 5 h. 6 a. 7 f. 8 e. 9 j.
10 g.

Practice

Idiomatic expressions
1 1 something that is easy to talk about but difficult to do
   2 to feel slightly ill
   3 to work hard during the day and stay up late at night in order to get everything done, usually resulting in mental and physical exhaustion
   4 to relax and not do very much
   5 to be extremely tired
   6 to be exhausted and unwell due to overwork or illness

   7 to feel unwell
   8 to feel completely well or healthy again after recovering from an illness or shock

2 a. 5, 7, and 4   b. 2 and 7   c. 1 d. 8 e. 6 and 3

4 a. someone who is ill but not expected to die, in a safe situation or place
   b. not in good physical form, not physically fit
   c. not in regular communication with something or someone and therefore without recent information or knowledge
   d. too far away to get
   e. to feel slightly unwell, not in one's usual good state of health
   f. impossible, not to be discussed at all, not worth considering

How multi-word verbs work

6 *to slow down* = to move or happen more slowly
   to bring something down = to reduce something
   to calm down = to become less angry, excited, or lively
   to die down = to become less intense
   to cool down = to become cooler or more calm
   to quieten down = to become less noisy

7 a. cool down   d. calm down/cool down
   b. bring down   e. quieten down
   c. slow down   f. die down

What's the answer?

1 a. *to pick up* a disease is about the moment of catching it; *to go down with* a disease is about the development of the symptoms and suffering from it.
   b. *to wake up* = to become conscious after being asleep
   to come round = to recover consciousness after fainting, being knocked out, or under anaesthetic.
   c. *to be worn out* = to be extremely tired, say, after a day at work; *to be run down* = to be exhausted and unwell because of too much work, or illness.

2 The opposite of *to pass out* is *to come round*.

Unit 4 A place of your own

Presentation

a. He found it through an agency. He came across an advertisement for flats while he was looking through the newspaper.
b. He took it because he liked it. He was getting on his parents' nerves and he wanted to be more independent.
c. He's going to convert the bedroom into a study and paint it blue.

d. He offers to put his friend up any time he is in London.

e. He invites his friend to a house-warming party.

Checking understanding

1 e. 2 f. 3 i. 4 g. 5 h. 6 b. 7 d. 8 a. 9 c.

Practice

a. on b. in c. on d. on e. in f. of g. for
h. with i. into j. through

How multi-word verbs work

a. *to brush up (on) something* = to improve knowledge or skills that have not been used for a while

b. *to train someone up* = to teach someone how to do something so that they reach a certain standard

c. *to read up (on) something* = to improve one's knowledge of something by reading a lot about it

d. *to smarten something up* = to make a place or person look neater and tidier

e. *to build something up* = to improve or develop something

What's the answer?

1 *to put someone up* = to give someone accommodation, but *to put something up* = to fix something in place (a picture, for example)

2 They all mean 'to pay a short informal visit', although *drop round/call round/drop over/call over* suggest an informal visit from someone who lives locally. All of them can be used intransitively, except for *to call on someone*, which must have an object.

Unit 5 Getting away from it all

Checking understanding

1 c. 2 h. 3 f. 4 e. 5 a. 6 g. 7 j. 8 i.
9 d. 10 b.

Practice

a. pick us up   d. set off   g. stop off
b. pick us up   e. get back   h. drop us off
c. look round   f. pick us up   i. get back

Idiomatic expressions

1 *It's just a stone's throw away.* = a very short distance from something

2 *Travel broadens the mind.* = experience of different places makes you more willing to accept and tolerate other people's beliefs and customs.

3 *to get away from it all* = to escape all one's daily worries and problems (by taking a holiday)

How multi-word verbs work

5 a. Type 3   e. Type 3   i. Type 1
   b. Type 3   f. Type 1   j. Type 3
   c. Type 1   g. Type 1
   d. Type 1   h. Type 1

6 Reciprocating (repeating a similar action)

ring/phone/call back   Mike phoned and asked you to phone him back later.

play something back   After we made the recording, we played it back to check it sounded all right.

shout back   He shouted at me so I shouted back at him.

What's the answer?

1 to check in at/to a hotel
  to touch down
  to drop someone off
  to get back from somewhere

2 *to go back* = to begin a return journey
  to get back = to arrive somewhere you started from
  When do you go back? = When do you begin your return journey?
  When do you get back? = When do you arrive at the place you started from?

3 *to get back* = to arrive at/return to where you started from after completing your journey, e.g. *He left New York on Monday, flew to England, stayed a few days and got back to New York on Friday.*
  to turn back = to return before completing a journey, e.g. *His plane left New York for England, but on the way it had engine problems, so it had to turn back. It didn't reach England.*

Unit 6 Family relationships

Presentation

1 They get on well with their parents.

2 Helen says her father is quite strict; David says their parents can be very strict; and the mother says they are reasonably strict.

3 The role of a parent is not easy because it involves a lot of worry. Children sometimes criticize their parents and sometimes won't listen to them. Good parents give their children love and confidence and they also set a good example.

Checking understanding

1 e. 2 g. 3 d. 4 a. 5 f. 6 h. 7 i. 8 j.
9 b. 10 c.

Practice

1 a. to dis/approve *of*
   someone/something
 b. to confide *in* someone
 c. to rely *on* someone
 d. to compare someone/
   something *with/to*
   someone/something

 e. to (dis)agree *with*
   someone; *with/about*
   something
 f. to argue *with* someone
   about something
 g. to worry *about*
   someone/something
 h. to listen *to* someone/
   something

Idiomatic expressions

2 1 *to see eye to eye* = to agree completely, have the
   same opinion
 2 *to have/get your own way* = to do what you want to
   do, often against the advice of others. Most often
   used in relation to children.
 3 *to be close to someone* = to like someone very much,
   have similar attitudes and emotions
 4 *to be the black sheep of the family* = someone whose
   conduct is considered to be a disgrace to the family
 5 *to take someone's side* = to support someone

 a. The problem is that she *has/gets her own way* all the
   time.
 b. My brother has always been *the black sheep* of the
   family.
 c. My grandparents always *took my side*.
 d. My father and I don't *see eye to eye* on politics.
 e. I *am very close to* my sister.

5 1 g. 2 f. 3 d. 4 b. 5 a. 6 e. 7 c.

What's the answer?

1 *to grow up* = to become adult and mature. It is a
  Type 1 multi-word verb.
  to bring someone up = to raise someone. It is a Type
  2 multi-word verb.
2 to look down on someone
3 a. She had a very strict upbringing.
  b. He doesn't behave in a very grown-up way.

Unit 7 You are what you wear

Presentation

a. So he could find out if other people were stupid or
  not and if they were good at their jobs. He also
  loved dressing up in beautiful clothes.
b. He wanted to know how they were getting on, and
  he wanted to send someone he could trust, so he
  chose a minister who was clever and good at his
  job.
c. He wanted to see if they were the right size.
d. They were pretending they could see the clothes
  because they didn't want to appear stupid and not
  good at their jobs.
e. Because there was no way out. He was pretending
  he could see the clothes too, because he thought
  everyone else could see them.
f. The innocent little boy simply described what he
  saw. In contrast to the adults, he was able to tell
  the truth because he had no fear of appearing
  stupid and had nothing to lose.
g. He didn't want to ruin the procession.
h. The story is saying many things:
  – People are too ready to accept what they think
    they ought to believe.
  – They don't trust their own common sense.
  – They are afraid to appear foolish.
  – People in positions of power are easily deceived
    and don't want to lose their jobs.

Checking understanding

1 g. 2 f. 3 b. 4 e. 5 c. 6 j. 7 i. 8 a.
9 d. 10 h.

Practice

1 a. about b. in c. in d. on e. of f. on g. in

4 a. out of stock b. out of luck c. out of this world
 d. out of date e. out of fashion

Idiomatic expressions

5 1 *a wolf in sheep's clothing* = Someone who pretends to
   be friendly in order to hide selfish or bad intentions.
 2 *There's no arguing about tastes.* = Everybody has
   different likes and dislikes, and taste is a very
   personal thing, so it is a waste of time to argue
   about it.
 3 *Beauty is only skin deep.* = A beautiful appearance
   can hide very different qualities.
 4 *You can't go by appearances.* = You can't judge
   someone by the way they dress, behave, or look.

5 *One man's meat is another man's poison.* = What is good or pleasing to one person may be bad or unsuitable for another.
6 *Beauty is in the eye of the beholder.* = Different people have different opinions about what is beautiful.

Numbers 2 and 5 are similar. And numbers 3, 4, and 6 are similar.

a. 2/5/6   b. 1   c. 4   d. 3/4

How multi-word verbs work
a. wash them up   b. tidy it up   c. Eat up
d. tidy up/clear up/clean up   e. dry them up

What's the answer?

1 – in fashion   – in stock
  – up to date/modern   – to put something on
  – in luck   – to undo something

2 *to go through with something* = to decide to do something, although it may be difficult or unpleasant; but *to carry on with something* = to continue with something you are already doing, despite difficulty or interruptions
3 *to take off* = to leave the ground and begin flying (Type 1, intransitive)
   to take something off = to undress (Type 2, transitive)

Unit 8 A narrow escape

Presentation

1 No one knows how the fire started. The hotel manager thought it was probably an accident. Perhaps someone was smoking in bed and fell asleep.
2 Some residents escaped via the roof and some were rescued by firefighters.

Checking understanding

1 c.   2 i.   3 a.   4 h.   5 g.   6 b.   7 d.   8 f.
9 j.   10 e.

Practice

a. on b. on/at c. in d. in e. under f. in g. from
h. by i. into

Idiomatic expressions
to have a narrow escape = to be very close to danger or something terrible but manage to escape
to be/go as white as a sheet = to be very pale in the face, especially because of illness or great fear

to shake life a leaf = to tremble with fear or great anxiety

3 a. The saucepan is *on fire*. The fire has *set off* the smoke detector. The woman is *calling out* for help. She will probably *call in* the fire brigade. The fire might spread to the curtains. She might try to *put out* the fire with an extinguisher.

b. The man is falling asleep. His cigarette might set fire to the bedclothes. A serious fire might *break out*. The smoke might *set off* the fire alarm. If the hotel fire alarm *goes off*, the fire brigade will be *called in*. The hotel will probably be in flames before they arrive. The hotel residents may need to *get out* of the building. The police will *look into* the causes of the fire.

c. The man is trapped and *calling out* for help. He is *going through* a terrible experience. The petrol might *burst into flames*. Someone in the street will probably *call in* the police and fire brigade. If the car is *on fire* when they arrive *on the scene*, they will try to *put it out*.

4 A plane was in serious trouble this morning when it tried to land at Heathrow. A fire *broke out* in one of its engines and soon the whole wing was *in flames*. The emergency services were *called out* and the plane made an emergency landing. The fire brigade soon had the situation *under control* and succeeded in *putting out* the fire before it spread to the rest of the plane. 'We *had a narrow escape*,' said one passenger. 'I never want to *go through* another experience like that again,' said another. Flight engineers are now *looking into* the cause of the fire.

burst into
5 to burst into tears/laughter/song/applause

How multi-word verbs work
6 a. Type 1   e. Type 2   i. Type 3
  b. Type 3   f. Type 3   j. Type 2
  c. Type 2   g. Type 1
  d. Type 1   h. Type 1

out
7 1 *to eat out* = to eat at a restaurant instead of at home
   to invite someone out = to ask someone to go with you to a play, party, etc.
   Note It is more formal than 'to take someone out'.
   to camp out = to sleep outdoors in a tent
   to stay out = to remain away from home, especially when you are expected to be there
   to take someone out = to invite and accompany someone to a place of entertainment or recreation and pay for them

2 *to leave someone/something out* = not include
someone/something in an activity or group
to keep someone/something out = to prevent
someone/something from entering a place or being
there
to shut someone/something out = to prevent
someone/something from entering a place by
shutting a door or window

What's the answer?

1 on purpose
2 out of control
3 'The police are in control' means the police are
controlling the situation, i.e. *to be in control* = to
control something. 'The situation is under control'
has a passive meaning, i.e. the situation is being
controlled by someone.
4 *to go off* is Type 1 and intransitive, e.g. an alarm bell
starts ringing by itself;
to set something off is Type 2 and transitive, e.g.
someone causes something else to start happening
5 *to set off* is Type 1, intransitive and means 'to begin
a journey'.

Unit 9 Getting on in life

Presentation

a. False. The company *cut back on* other staff to save
money. He lost his job when the company *closed
down*.
b. True. It *closed down* because times were hard.
c. False. The companies *turned him down*.
d. True. They *took him on*.
e. True. He wanted her to *get on in life*.
f. False. She was told she would soon *pick it up*.
g. True. It *took up* a lot of her time.
h. False. She earned enough money to *get by*.
i. False. Everything about her job *got her down*.
j. True. She decided to *go in for* law.

Checking understanding

1 i. 2 c. 3 h. 4 f. 5 j. 6 a. 7 e. 8 d.
9 b. 10 g.

Practice

1 a. as b. for c. onto/for d. in e. in f. off
g. to h. to i. to j. on k. psychiatrist

Idiomatic expressions

2 1 *to get on in life/in the world* = to be successful, to
improve one's financial and social status
2 *to be cut out for something* = to have the right
qualities and abilities for a job, to be naturally well
suited for something. **Note** We can say 'I'm not cut
out for teaching' or 'I'm not cut out to be a teacher'
3 *to say something point-blank* = to say something
directly, even rudely, without any explanation or
apologies
4 *That's the last straw!* = an additional problem to an
already difficult situation which makes it intolerable.
As a result you take action (e.g. you complain,
resign, lose your temper, etc.). The complete
expression is 'It is the last straw that breaks the
camel's back'.
5 *to make one's way in the world* = to be successful
(same as 1 above)
6 *The world is one's oyster.* = you can do anything, go
anywhere (because you are young, successful and/or
rich).

a. cut out for   b. get on in life/the world
c. was her oyster   d. That's the last straw!
e. point-blank; point-blank.

4 1 policeman   2 nurse   3 taxi-driver   4 actor
5 flight attendant   6 doctor   7 school teacher

How multi-word verbs work

5 a. with   b. with   c. on   d. of   e. with
f. on   g. on   h. with

What's the answer?

1 CLOSING DOWN SALE
2 *to start (something) up* (to start up a business)
to open (something) up (to open up a shop)

3
look	read
hold	smarten
give	build
pick	bring
wake	grow
get	dress
keep	drink
catch	eat
put	tidy
take	wash
brighten	dry
do	clean
brush	clear
train	make

Unit 10 A nightmare journey

Presentation

1 e.   2 c.   3 a.   4 d.   5 g.   6 b.   7 f.

Checking understanding

1 f.   2 j.   3 d.   4 i.   5 g.   6 c.   7 h.   8 e.
9 b.   10 a.

Practice

1   1 pull up   2 pull over   3 pull out   4 pull out

2   a.   on   d.   for
    b.   on   e.   for
    c.   about/of   f.   for (something)

3   a.   without fail   d.   wrong with, beyond
    b.   under repair   repair
    c.   without success   e.   without warning

Time expressions

5   *on time* = to be punctual, to happen at the right time
    (e.g. a train that leaves at the time given on a
    timetable). If something is not on time, it is late.
    in time = to be early enough to do something. If
    something does not happen in time, it is too late to
    do something.
    just in time = to have only just enough time to do
    something
    in no time (at all) = very quickly, soon

    a. on time   b. in time/just in time
    c. in no time at all   d. in time   e. just in time

Idiomatic expressions

6   1 *to make up for lost time* = to make a special effort to
      compensate for time lost earlier
    2 *My patience is running out.* = My patience is nearly
      exhausted.
    3 *I'll keep my fingers crossed for you.* = to wish someone
      good luck and success in an interview or exam
    4 *Better late than never.* = It's better that something
      should happen late or arrive late rather than not at
      all.
    5 *It's better to be safe than sorry.* = It's better to be
      careful and avoid danger rather than take risks.

How multi-word verbs work

7   a.   turn it up   d.   warm it up/heat it up
    b.   going up   e.   build up
    c.   speak up   f.   put up

8   a.   take off   d.   set off
    b.   sailed off   e.   fly off
    c.   ran off   f.   rode off

What's the answer?

to be short of something = not have enough of
something (food, money, time)
to be out of something = to have nothing left

Unit 11 What's in the news?

Checking understanding

1 b. (or 1 i.)   2 i. (or 2 b.)   3 f.   4 e.   5 j.
6 g.   7 h.   8 c.   9 a.   10 d.

Practice

1   a. in   b. on   c. on   d. on   e. on   f. on

2   a. for   b. with   c. to   d. of   e. of   f. of   g. to

3   **Picture 1** He's *breaking into* a house. He might *get away*
    with some valuable things or he might get *picked up*
    by the police and *charged with robbery.*
    Picture 2 They've just *held up* a jeweller's shop. They
    are going to *make off* in a car. They might *get away*
    with the jewels.
    Picture 3 Perhaps the police are going to *arrest*
    someone for a crime. Perhaps someone has *accused*
    him of something, or he is going to be *charged with*
    something. The man might try to *make off.*
    Picture 4 Someone has *broken into* a bank and *blown*
    up the safe. They *got away with* the money.
    Picture 5 Some people have been *cut off* by floods. The
    emergency services were *standing by* and now they
    are *picking up* the people. The people have *been*
    through a frightening experience.
    Picture 6 Perhaps these two men were *put on trial* for
    robbery, *convicted of* the crime, and *sentenced to*
    several years in prison. Now they are trying to *break*
    out of prison. Perhaps they will *make off* in a stolen
    car. They will be *on the run* from the police.

Idiomatic expression

4   *Crime doesn't pay* = crime does not provide you with
    any real profit because you are usually caught and
    punished in the end.

5   a. BREAK-IN   b. HOLD-UP   c. BREAKOUT
    d. CUTBACK   e. CUT-OUT

What's the answer?

1   *to blow up* = to explode. Type 1, intransitive
    to blow something up = to destroy something with
    explosives. Type 2, transitive

2 *to pick someone/something up* = 1 to catch an illness
2 to collect someone/something 3 to arrest someone
4 to rescue someone

Unit 12 Across a crowded room

Presentation

1 1 a.   2 h.   3 f.   4 i.   5 c.   6 g.   7 l.   8 b.
9 d.   10 k.   11 e.   12 j.

Checking understanding

1 c.   2 j.   3 f.   4 b.   5 a.   6 i.   7 h.   8 e.
9 d.   10 g.

Practice

1 fallen out   going on at   going off   going out with
found out   going out with   break off   called ... off
broken up   get over

There are plenty more fish in the sea. = There are plenty
of other people to meet. This is often said to try to
comfort (usually unsuccessfully!) someone who has just
lost a partner.

2 keen on   fond of   in love with her   in common
engaged to   married to

Idiomatic expressions

4 1 love at first sight   2 to be head over heels in love
3 to drown your sorrows

5 1 *the eternal triangle* = a situation of emotional conflict
in which two men love the same woman, or two
women love the same man
2 *an old flame* = a former boyfriend or girlfriend,
someone with whom you once had a romantic
relationship
3 *a one-sided relationship* = a relationship in which one
of the two people feels and does much more than
the other
4 *There's no love lost between them* = two people or
groups who greatly dislike one another
5 *a love–hate relationship* = a relationship in which
there are strong feelings of both love and hate

How multi-word verbs work

6 a. turn off/switch off   b. cut off   c. put it off
d. ring off   e. is off

What's the answer?

1 *to break up* is used intransitively: 'The marriage
broke up'. It is a Type 1 multi-word verb. *To break
something off* is similar in meaning but it is used to
suggest someone has taken action to end something
It is used transitively: 'She broke off the
relationship'. It is a Type 2 multi-word verb.
2 *to put something off* = to postpone something; *to call
something off* = to cancel something
3 *to break off* = to discontinue something that is
actually happening or already exists (an
engagement), whereas *to call off* is to cancel
something that is planned for the future